Getting Ready for High-Stakes Assessment

Grade 8

Contents

About *Getting Ready for High-Stakes Assessment*

This *Getting Ready for High-Stakes Assessment* print guide consists of standards-based practice and practice tests.

Standards-Based Practice

The items in each practice set are designed to give students exposure to the wide variety of ways in which a standard may be assessed.

All standards-based practice sets are available to students online. Online item types include traditional multiple choice as well as technology-enhanced item types that are similar to the ones students will see on actual high-stakes assessments. The online practice experience also offers students hints, corrective feedback, and opportunities to try an item multiple times. You can assign online standards-based practice and receive instant access to student data and reports. The reports can help you pinpoint student strengths and weaknesses and tailor instruction to meet their needs. The standards-based practice sets in this guide mirror those found online; however, some technology-enhanced item types have been modified or replaced with items suitable for paper-and-pencil testing.

Practice Tests

Into Math also includes three practice tests. The practice tests are available online. Online item types include traditional multiple choice as well as technology-enhanced item types that are similar to ones students will see on actual high-stakes assessments. You can assign the online tests for instant access to data and standards alignments. The practice tests in this guide mirror those found online; however, some technology-enhanced item types were modified or replaced with items suitable for paper-and-pencil testing. This guide includes record forms for these tests that show the content focus and depth of knowledge for each item.

Assessment Item Types

High-stakes assessments contain item types beyond the traditional multiple-choice format. This allows for a more robust assessment of students' understanding of concepts and skills. High-stakes assessments are administered via computers, and *Into Math* presents items in formats similar to what students will see on the real tests. The following information is provided to help you familiarize your students with these different types of items. An example of each item type appears on the following pages. You may want to use the examples to introduce the item types to students. These pages describe the most common item types. You may find other types on some tests.

Example 1: Multiselect

Upon first glance, many students may easily confuse this item type with a traditional multiple-choice item. Explain to students that this type of item will have a special direction line that asks them to select all the answers to the problem that are correct.

Which of these represents a proportional relationship?

Select **all** the correct answers.

(A) $y = \frac{1}{2}x$ (D) $y = 3x^2$

(B) $y = 2x$ (E) $y = 1 - x$

(C) $y = 2x + 1$

Example 2: Fill in the Blank

Sometimes when students take a digital test, they will have to select a word, number, or symbol from a drop-down list or drag answer options into blanks. The print versions of the *Into Math* tests ask students to write the correct answer in the blank.

Leo bought 3 apples and 4 pears. Fill in the blanks with the correct ratios from the list.

The ratio of apples to pears Leo bought is _____.

The ratio of pears to total pieces of fruit Leo bought is _____.

| 4:3 | 3:7 | 7:3 | 4:7 | 3:4 | 7:4 |

© Houghton Mifflin Harcourt Publishing Company

Example 3: Classification

Some *Into Math* assessment items require students to categorize numbers or shapes. Digital versions of this item type require students to drag answer options into the correct place in a table. When the classification involves more complex equations or drawings, each object will have a letter next to it. Print versions of this item type will ask students to write answer options in the correct place in the table. Tell students that sometimes they may write the same number or word in more than one column of the table.

Write each fraction in the correct place in the table.

Equivalent to a Repeating Decimal	Equivalent to a Terminating Decimal

$\frac{2}{3}$ $\frac{1}{8}$ $\frac{5}{13}$ $\frac{27}{45}$ $-\frac{3}{14}$

Example 4: Matching

In some items, students will need to match one set of objects to another. In some computer-based items, students will need to drag an answer option into a box next to the element it matches. On paper-based tests, they do this by drawing a line connecting the two elements that match.

Draw a line from each unit rate to the situation it matches.

10 pounds for $45	$5.25 per pound
8 pounds for $42	$4.80 per pound
5 pounds for $24	$4.50 per pound
12 pounds for $66	$5.50 per pound

Example 5: Choice Matrix

Students may also need to match elements by filling in a table. On the digital tests, they select buttons in the table to indicate the correct answers. On paper-based tests, they place X's in the table to indicate the correct answers.

Place an X in the table to show whether each number is rational or irrational.

	Rational	Irrational
$-\frac{1}{2}$		
$\sqrt{10}$		
$\sqrt{25}$		
π		

Example 6: Graphing/Number Line

On computerized tests, students will be expected to use a graphing tool to plot points, graph lines, and draw polygons. On paper-based versions of these items, students will plot, graph, or draw on a grid or number line supplied with the item.

Graph the proportional relationship $y = 3x$.

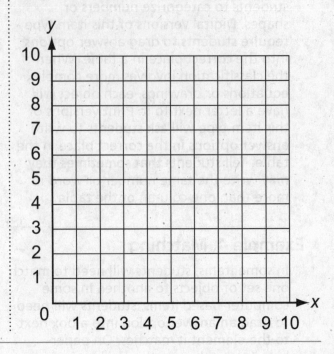

Example 7: Ordering

Ordering items allow students to drag and drop elements into the correct order within a list. In the print versions of these items, students write the elements in the correct order on the lines provided.

Write the numbers on the lines in the correct order from **GREATEST** to **LEAST**.

| -1.5 | 4 | 0 | -0.9 | -2.2 |

_____ _____ _____ _____ _____

1 A diagram showing the relationships between different types of numbers is shown.

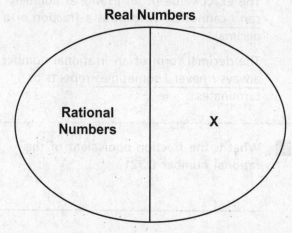

Real Numbers

Rational Numbers

X

Which label could replace X in the diagram?

Ⓐ irrational numbers

Ⓑ negative integers

Ⓒ positive integers

Ⓓ whole numbers

2 Which statement is false?

Ⓐ At least some integers are irrational.

Ⓑ At least some real numbers are irrational.

Ⓒ At least some integers are whole numbers.

Ⓓ At least some rational numbers are integers.

3 What is the fraction equivalent of the rational number 0.$\overline{54}$?

Ⓐ $\frac{27}{50}$

Ⓑ $\frac{109}{200}$

Ⓒ $\frac{6}{11}$

Ⓓ $\frac{5}{4}$

4 Which number is a rational number?

Ⓐ $\sqrt{56}$

Ⓑ $\sqrt{63}$

Ⓒ $\sqrt{196}$

Ⓓ $\sqrt{240}$

5 Which set of numbers does not include any integers?

Ⓐ counting numbers

Ⓑ irrational numbers

Ⓒ positive numbers

Ⓓ whole numbers

6 When the fraction $\frac{11}{30}$ is expressed in decimal form, what is the repeating digit?

7 How many digits are there in the repeating block for the decimal equivalent of $\frac{3}{7}$?

8 Place an X in the table to show whether each fraction equals a repeating decimal.

	Yes	No
$\frac{18}{81}$		
$\frac{11}{88}$		
$\frac{4}{6}$		
$\frac{6}{30}$		

9 Place an X in the table to show whether each fraction has a decimal equivalent that repeats or terminates.

	Repeating Decimal	Terminating Decimal
$-\dfrac{41}{33}$		
$-\dfrac{112}{90}$		
$-\dfrac{31}{25}$		
$-\dfrac{128}{125}$		

10 Place an X in the table to classify each number as rational or irrational.

	Rational	Irrational
$0.0\overline{8}$		
$-\dfrac{3}{4}$		
$\sqrt{6}$		
2.2235		

11 Write the number $0.6\overline{2}$ as a fraction in simplest form.

_____

12 Circle the correct answers to complete the sentences.

The exact value of an irrational number can / cannot be written as a fraction or a decimal.

The decimal form of an irrational number always / never / sometimes repeats or terminates.

13 What is the fraction equivalent of the rational number $0.\overline{321}$?

_____

14 What is the decimal equivalent of the rational number $-\dfrac{3}{8}$?

_____

15 Write the number 0.48 as a fraction in simplest form.

_____

1 Between which two integers does the value of $\sqrt{50}$ lie?

(A) 7 and 8

(B) 8 and 9

(C) 24 and 26

(D) 49 and 51

---

2 A number line with the points A, B, C, and D labeled is shown.

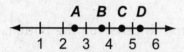

Which lettered point could show the position of $\sqrt{20}$ on the number line?

(A) A

(B) B

(C) C

(D) D

---

3 Between which pair of decimals does $\sqrt{13}$ fall on a number line?

(A) 3.0 and 3.1

(B) 3.5 and 3.6

(C) 3.6 and 3.7

(D) 3.9 and 4.0

---

4 The number e is an irrational number approximately equal to 2.718.

Between which pair of square roots does e fall?

(A) $\sqrt{2}$ and $\sqrt{3}$

(B) $\sqrt{4}$ and $\sqrt{5}$

(C) $\sqrt{7}$ and $\sqrt{8}$

(D) $\sqrt{8}$ and $\sqrt{9}$

5 What is an estimate of $\sqrt{35}$, to the nearest tenth?

_____

6 Estimate $\sqrt{250}$ to two decimal places.

_____

7 Write the values in the boxes in order from GREATEST on the top to LEAST on the bottom.

$\sqrt{150}$	
$11\frac{4}{9}$	
4π	
$2\sqrt{35}$	

8 Which numbers are between $\frac{17}{4}$ and $\sqrt{20}$?

Select **all** that apply.

Ⓐ $\sqrt{34} - 1.5$

Ⓑ $\pi + 1.2$

Ⓒ $1 + \sqrt{8}$

Ⓓ $\frac{5\pi}{3}$

Ⓔ $\frac{\sqrt{75}}{2}$

9 Plot the approximate position of the point $\sqrt{87}$.

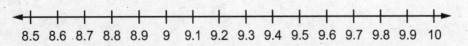

8.5 8.6 8.7 8.8 8.9 9 9.1 9.2 9.3 9.4 9.5 9.6 9.7 9.8 9.9 10

10 What integer lies between $\frac{4\pi}{3}$ and $\sqrt{30}$?

_____

© Houghton Mifflin Harcourt Publishing Company

1 Which expression represents 64?

Ⓐ 2^5

Ⓑ 2^6

Ⓒ 2^7

Ⓓ 2^8

2 What is an equivalent expression for $11^2 \times 11^5$?

Ⓐ 11^7

Ⓑ 11^{10}

Ⓒ 121^7

Ⓓ 121^{10}

3 What is an equivalent expression for $\frac{13^9}{13^6}$?

Ⓐ 1^{-3}

Ⓑ 1^3

Ⓒ 13^{-3}

Ⓓ 13^3

4 What is an equivalent expression for $(9^4)^6$?

Ⓐ 9^{24}

Ⓑ 9^{10}

Ⓒ $\frac{1}{9^2}$

Ⓓ 9^2

5 What is the simplified form of the expression $(8^5)^0 + (7 + 3)^6 \times 10^{-8}$?

Ⓐ $\frac{1}{100}$

Ⓑ $1\frac{1}{100}$

Ⓒ 100

Ⓓ 101

6 Which **four** of the following expressions have a value less than 1?

Ⓐ $\frac{4^{11}}{4^{14}}$

Ⓑ $\frac{(3^5)^2}{3^8}$

Ⓒ $4^{-1} \times 4^5$

Ⓓ $(2^3)^{-2}$

Ⓔ $(5^4)^2 \times 5^{-11}$

Ⓕ $\frac{6^{-4} \times 6^6}{6^3}$

7 Place an X in the table to show whether properties of exponents are used correctly to simplify each expression.

	Yes	No
$\frac{5^{10}}{5^5} = 5^2$		
$(4^8)^3 = 4^{24}$		
$10^{-4} = \frac{1}{4^{10}}$		
$15^6 \times 15^3 = 15^{18}$		
$(6^8)^0 = 1$		

8 Find the missing exponent.

$$\frac{5^{11}}{5^{\square}} = 5^4$$

9 Fill in the blanks with the correct answers from the list to complete the sentence.

The expression $\frac{(14^2)^4}{14^8}$ represents a number that is _____ 1 because the simplified exponent is _____.

less than	equal to	greater than
negative	0	positive

10 Place an X in the table to show each pair of equivalent expressions.

	8^{-14}	8^{-9}	8^{-4}	8^{20}
$(8^{-5})^2 \times \dfrac{8^{12}}{8^6}$				
$\dfrac{8^{11} \times 8^5}{8^{-4}}$				
$\dfrac{1}{8^{-3}} \times (8^2)^{-6}$				
$\dfrac{8^{-7} \times 8^6}{(8^{-1})^{-13}}$				

1 What is the value of $\sqrt{\frac{1}{4}}$?

Ⓐ $-\frac{1}{2}$

Ⓑ $\frac{1}{8}$

Ⓒ $\frac{1}{2}$

Ⓓ 2

2 Which value of x is a solution to $x^2 = 10$?

Ⓐ $\sqrt{10}$

Ⓑ 5

Ⓒ $\sqrt{20}$

Ⓓ 100

3 What is the value of $\sqrt[3]{\frac{8}{27}}$?

Ⓐ $\frac{2}{9}$

Ⓑ $\frac{2}{3}$

Ⓒ $\frac{3}{2}$

Ⓓ $\frac{9}{2}$

4 Which value of x is a solution to $x^3 = 100$?

Ⓐ $\sqrt[3]{33.3}$

Ⓑ $\sqrt[3]{100}$

Ⓒ 10

Ⓓ 300

5 Colin has a square garden with an area of 97 square feet. What is the length of each side of the garden?

Ⓐ $\sqrt[3]{97}$ ft

Ⓑ 9 ft

Ⓒ $\sqrt{97}$ ft

Ⓓ 10 ft

6 Which numbers have irrational square roots?

Select **all** the correct answers.

Ⓐ 1

Ⓑ 2

Ⓒ 3

Ⓓ 4

Ⓔ 5

7 Fill in the correct numbers from the list into each box next to its equivalent radical expression.

 $\sqrt{4}$

 $\sqrt{81}$

 $\sqrt[3]{\frac{1}{64}}$

 $\sqrt[3]{-\frac{1}{8}}$

| $-\frac{1}{2}$ | $\frac{1}{2}$ | $-\frac{1}{4}$ | $\frac{1}{4}$ | 2 | 9 | $\frac{1}{8}$ | $-\frac{1}{8}$ | -9 | -2 |

8 Monica's rectangular living room is 12 ft by 15 ft. She has a square rug that covers $\frac{5}{9}$ of the area of the floor. What is the side length of the square rug in feet?

_____

9 Terry has two square sheets of wrapping paper. The area of the first sheet of wrapping paper is 36 in.^{2} The side length of the second sheet of wrapping paper is 1 in. longer than that of the first. Find the side length of the larger sheet of wrapping paper in inches.

_____

10 A rectangular prism measures 2 in. by 4 in. by 8 in. What is the side length in inches of a cube with the same volume?

_____

11 The volume of a cube-shaped vase is 216 in.^{3} How long is each side of the vase in inches?

_____

12 Katherine is building a square-shaped frame for a window. The area of the window is 196 square inches.

Part A

Which equation can Katherine use to find the length of each side of the window, x?

Ⓐ $x^3 = 196$

Ⓑ $4x = 196$

Ⓒ $196 = 2x$

Ⓓ $196 = x^2$

Part B

How long is each side of the frame in inches that Katherine makes for the window?

_____

1 What is 12,325 written in scientific notation?

(A) 1.2325×10^{-4}

(B) 12.325×10^{3}

(C) 1.2325×10^{4}

(D) 12.325×10^{-3}

2 What is 0.005007 written in scientific notation?

(A) 5.007×10^{3}

(B) 5.007×10^{-3}

(C) 5.007×10^{-4}

(D) 5.007×10^{4}

3 What is 1.0315×10^{6} written in standard notation?

(A) 1,031,500

(B) 103,150

(C) 0.000010315

(D) 0.0000010315

4 What is 9.2568×10^{-3} written in standard notation?

(A) 0.0092568

(B) 0.092568

(C) 925.68

(D) 9,256.8

5 What is 8.305×10^{-7} written in standard notation?

(A) −830,500,000

(B) −83,050,000

(C) 0.0000008305

(D) 0.00000008305

6 Select the **three** statements that are true.

(A) 3×10^4 is 50 times as much as 6×10^2.

(B) 5×10^2 is 100 times as much as 5×10^{-2}.

(C) 7×10^{-5} is 5,000 times as much as 1.4×10^{-9}.

(D) 8×10^{-12} is 0.0001 times as much as 8×10^{-8}.

(E) 2×10^{-6} is 0.01 times as much as 2×10^{-4}.

(F) 1.8×10^{-3} is 0.0000002 times as much as 9×10^4.

7 Which **two** of the following measurements are equal to 0.000043 L?

(A) 4.3×10^2 L

(B) 4.3×10^{-4} L

(C) 4.3×10^{-5} L

(D) 4.3×10^5 mL

(E) 4.3×10^{-2} mL

(F) 4.3×10^{-3} mL

8 A business sold for $32.6 million. Write that number in scientific notation.

9 Alea and Carlos are at the beach trying to guess the number of grains of sand. Alea estimates that there are 5×10^{15} grains of sand on the beach. Carlos estimates that there are 2×10^{12} grains of sand. How many times greater is Alea's estimate than Carlos's estimate?

_____ times greater

10 A water sample taken from city A had 6.28×10^6 bacteria per liter. A water sample taken from city B had 1.256×10^5 bacteria per liter. How many times greater is the bacteria level in city A's water sample than the bacteria level in city B's water sample?

_____ times greater

1 What is $3.75 \times 10^7 + 7.1 \times 10^6$ in scientific notation?

- Ⓐ 44.6×10^6
- Ⓑ 4.46×10^7
- Ⓒ 10.85×10^{13}
- Ⓓ 1.085×10^{14}

2 What is $0.073 - 5.1 \times 10^{-3}$ in scientific notation?

- Ⓐ -50.27×10^{-4}
- Ⓑ -5.027×10^{-3}
- Ⓒ 67.9×10^{-3}
- Ⓓ 6.79×10^{-2}

3 What is $(8.4 \times 10^4)(9.5 \times 10^3)$ in scientific notation?

- Ⓐ 79.8×10^7
- Ⓑ 7.98×10^8
- Ⓒ 79.8×10^{12}
- Ⓓ 7.98×10^{13}

4 What is $\dfrac{6.25 \times 10^{-6}}{12.5}$ in scientific notation?

- Ⓐ 5×10^{-7}
- Ⓑ 0.5×10^{-6}
- Ⓒ 2×10^{-6}
- Ⓓ 0.2×10^{-5}

5 What is $(4.1 \times 10^{-3})(3.2 \times 10^{-2})$ in standard form?

- Ⓐ 0.0001312
- Ⓑ 0.00001312
- Ⓒ $1,312,000$
- Ⓓ $13,120,000$

6 Which values are equivalent to $0.35 + 1.5 \times 10^{-3}$?

Select **all** the correct answers.

- (A) 0.00185
- (B) 0.3515
- (C) 1500.35
- (D) 1.85×10^{-3}
- (E) 3.5×10^{-1}
- (F) 1.50035×10^3

---

7 Which values are equivalent to $\dfrac{0.75}{2.5 \times 10^6}$?

Select **all** the correct answers.

- (A) 0.0000003
- (B) 0.000003
- (C) 300,000
- (D) 3×10^{-7}
- (E) 3×10^{-6}
- (F) 3×10^5

---

8 A rectangular-shaped electric component measures 1.2×10^{-5} m long by 1.5×10^{-4} meters wide. What is the area of the component in square meters? Express the answer in scientific notation.

---

9 What is the simplified form of $\dfrac{3 \times 10^{-3} + 6 \times 10^{-2}}{(7 \times 10^4)(3 \times 10^8)}$?

Express the answer in scientific notation.

---

10 If an airplane travels halfway around the world, flying just above the Equator, it would travel approximately 1.25×10^4 miles. How many miles would a plane travel if it flew around the world, just above the Equator, $3\frac{1}{2}$ times? Express the answer in standard form.

1 The graph shows a proportional relationship.

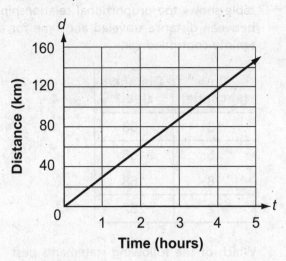

Time (hours)

What is the unit rate shown by the graph?

Ⓐ 30 hours per kilometer

Ⓑ 30 kilometers per hour

Ⓒ 60 hours per kilometer

Ⓓ 60 kilometers per hour

2 The cost, C, in dollars of a prepaid cell phone call is proportional to the time t, in minutes, that the call lasts. The equation that represents this relationship for carrier A is $C = 0.15t$. The table shows the relationship for carrier B.

Time (minutes)	Cost (dollars)
2	0.24
5	0.60
10	1.20
30	3.60

Which carrier has a lower unit rate?

Ⓐ carrier A

Ⓑ carrier B

Ⓒ Carrier A and carrier B have the same unit rate.

Ⓓ The relationship cannot be determined.

3 The number of pages that a laser printer prints is proportional to the printing time in minutes. Printer A prints 104 pages in 4 minutes. The table shows the relationship between the amount of time and the number of pages printed for printer B.

Time (minutes)	Pages Printed
3	84
5	140
9	252
14	392

Which printer prints more slowly?

Ⓐ printer A

Ⓑ printer B

Ⓒ Printer A and printer B have the same unit rate.

Ⓓ The relationship cannot be determined.

4 Which of the following proportional situations could be represented by this graph?

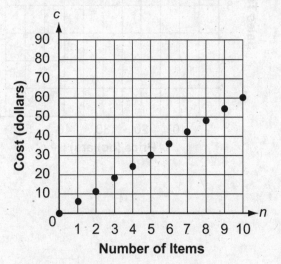

Number of Items

Select the **three** correct answers.

Ⓐ 2 pairs of headphones cost $12

Ⓑ 24 carrots cost $4

Ⓒ 3 packs of D batteries cost $18

Ⓓ 6 bags of apples cost $36

Ⓔ 6 jigsaw puzzles cost $10

5 The table below shows the proportional relationship between an item's price in dollars and the sales tax in dollars charged for that item.

Price (dollars)	Sales Tax (dollars)
14	1.12
24	1.92
30	2.40
44	3.52

Graph the line that represents the relationship.

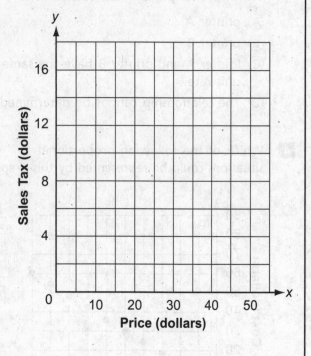

6 A remote-controlled truck travels at a constant rate of 108 feet in 6 seconds. The table shows the proportional relationship between distance traveled and time for a remote-controlled car.

Time (seconds)	Distance (feet)
3	63
5	105
8	168
12	252

Which of the following statements best describes the relationship between the speed of the truck and the speed of the car?

Ⓐ The remote control car travels at a faster rate of 18 feet per second.

Ⓑ The remote control car travels at a faster rate of 21 feet per second.

Ⓒ The remote control truck travels at a faster rate of 18 feet per second.

Ⓓ The remote control truck travels at a faster rate of 21 feet per second.

7 Johan is comparing energy consumption for two different brands of refrigerators. The energy consumed, e, in watts is proportional to the time, t, in hours that the refrigerator is operating. The equation $e = 160t$ models the relationship for brand R. Another refrigerator, brand S, consumes energy at a constant rate of 435 watts in 3 hours. Which brand consumes less energy per hour?

Ⓐ Brand R consumes less energy at the rate of 145 watts per hour.

Ⓑ Brand R consumes less energy at the rate of 160 watts per hour.

Ⓒ Brand S consumes less energy at the rate of 145 watts per hour.

Ⓓ Brand S consumes less energy at the rate of 160 watts per hour.

1 The graph of a line is shown.

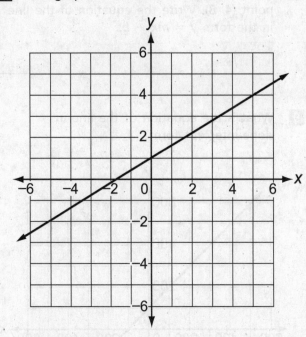

Why is the slope of the line the same between any two distinct points on the line?

(A) because all right triangles that have a vertical leg, a horizontal leg, and a portion of the line as the hypotenuse are similar, so the ratio of the length of the vertical leg to the length of the horizontal leg is always $\frac{5}{3}$

(B) because all right triangles that have a vertical leg, a horizontal leg, and a portion of the line as the hypotenuse are similar, so the ratio of the length of the vertical leg to the length of the horizontal leg is always $\frac{3}{5}$

(C) because all right triangles that have a vertical leg, a horizontal leg, and a portion of the line as the hypotenuse are congruent, so the ratio of the length of the vertical leg to the length of the horizontal leg is always $\frac{5}{3}$

(D) because all right triangles that have a vertical leg, a horizontal leg, and a portion of the line as the hypotenuse are congruent, so the ratio of the length of the vertical leg to the length of the horizontal leg is always $\frac{3}{5}$

2 A line passes through the points $(0, -4)$ and $(2, -11)$. If (x, y) is an arbitrary point on the line other than $(0, -4)$, which equation can you write for the line based on the fact that the slope of a line is constant?

(A) $\dfrac{y - 0}{x - (-4)} = -\dfrac{7}{2}$

(B) $\dfrac{y - 0}{x - (-4)} = -\dfrac{2}{7}$

(C) $\dfrac{y - (-4)}{x - 0} = -\dfrac{7}{2}$

(D) $\dfrac{y - (-4)}{x - 0} = -\dfrac{2}{7}$

3 A line that has a slope of $-\dfrac{5}{6}$ passes through the origin. Let (x, y) be an arbitrary point on the line other than the origin. Which of the following equations properly uses the fact that the slope of a line is constant to derive an equation of the line?

(A) $\dfrac{y}{x} = -\dfrac{5}{6}$

(B) $\dfrac{y}{x} = \dfrac{5}{6}$

(C) $\dfrac{x}{y} = \dfrac{5}{6}$

(D) $\dfrac{x}{y} = -\dfrac{5}{6}$

4 For the line that passes through $(0, 5)$ and has a slope of -3, you use the fact that the slope of a line is constant to derive the equation $\dfrac{y - 5}{x - 0} = -3$. What is an equivalent form of this equation?

(A) $y = 3x - 5$

(B) $y = 3x + 5$

(C) $y = -3x - 5$

(D) $y = -3x + 5$

5 What is the slope of a line that passes through the points (9, 8) and (2, 3)?

(A) $-\dfrac{7}{5}$

(B) $-\dfrac{5}{7}$

(C) $\dfrac{5}{7}$

(D) $\dfrac{7}{5}$

6 What is the slope of the line that passes through the points (3, 7) and (7, 14)?

$m = $ _____

7 What is the equation of the line in slope-intercept form?

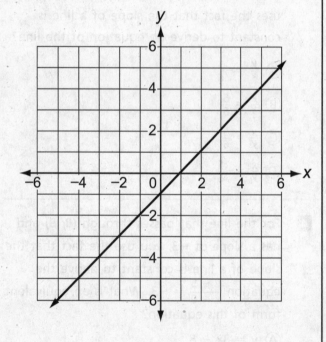

_____

8 A line passes through the origin and the point (4, 8). Write the equation of the line in the form $y = mx + b$.

_____

9 What is the equation of the line in slope-intercept form?

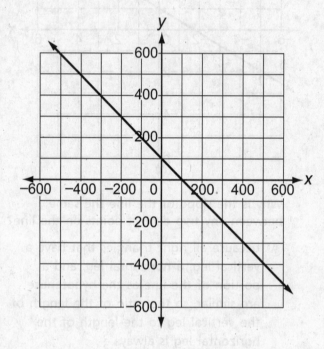

_____

10 What is the equation of the line that passes through the points (4, 2) and (8, 4) in slope-intercept form?

_____

1 How many solutions does the equation
$5x + 17 = 4(3x - 1)$ have?

(A) infinitely many solutions

(B) one solution

(C) no solutions

(D) cannot be determined

2 How many solutions does the equation
$7x - 11 = 5(x - 2) + 2x - 1$ have?

(A) infinitely many solutions

(B) one solution

(C) no solutions

(D) cannot be determined

3 Which of the following equations has
exactly one solution?

(A) $-7x + 2 = -3(x - 3) - 4x - 7$

(B) $14x = 7(2x + 2)$

(C) $5x + 3 = -2(2x + 3)$

(D) $3(4x + 2) - 9 = 12x - 3$

4 What is a possible result of simplifying the
equation $15x - 4 = 3(5x - 4)$?

(A) $-4 = -4$

(B) $x = 4$

(C) $-4 = -12$

(D) $x = 0$

5 For how many values of k does the
equation $kx + 4 = 2x + 3$ have no
solutions?

(A) one

(B) two

(C) three

(D) four

6 Which of the following equations has
no solutions?

(A) $-6x + 1 = -3(2x + 1) + x$

(B) $-5 + 14x = 7(2x) - 5$

(C) $4x - 4 = -4(-x + 1)$

(D) $-9x + 2 = -3(3x + 2)$

7 Select **all** the equations that have no
solutions.

(A) $7x - 9 = 47$

(B) $6x - 9 = 3(2x - 3)$

(C) $-2x + 10 = 2(-x + 5) + 1$

(D) $-x + 20 = x - 4$

(E) $-5x - 5 = -5(x - 1)$

8 Suppose a linear equation in one variable,
x, is simplified. Select **all** the resulting
equations that would indicate that the
original equation has infinitely many solutions.

(A) $-4 = -4$ (D) $x = 0$

(B) $11 = x$ (E) $1 = -1$

(C) $0 = 0$ (F) $x = x$

9 Patrick solved an equation as shown.

$-3(5 - x) + 2x = 5(x - 3)$

$-15 - 3x + 2x = 5x - 15$

$-15 - x = 5x - 15$

$-x = 5x$

$-6x = 0$

$x = 0$

Which statement is correct?

(A) He made a mistake. The equation has
no solutions.

(B) He did not make a mistake. The
equation has no solutions.

(C) He did not make a mistake. The
equation has one solution.

(D) He made a mistake. The equation has
infinitely many solutions.

Name _____

10 Place an X in the table to show the number of solutions for each equation.

	One Solution	No Solutions	Infinitely Many Solutions
$7x + 5 = 2(4x + 3)$			
$x - 2(x - 6) = -x + 12$			
$8x + 5 = 5x - 7$			
$2(x - 1) = 3(x - 4)$			
$4x - 1 = 2(2x - 1)$			

11 What values of a and b would make the equation shown have infinitely many solutions?

$a(x - 5) = 5x - b$

$a = $ _____ and $b = $ _____

12 Place an X in the table to show the number of solutions for each equation.

	One Solution	No Solutions	Infinitely Many Solutions
$2(x - 7) = -3(x - 6)$			
$14 - 3x - 5 = 3(x + 3)$			
$12x - 1 = 6(2x - 1)$			
$-x(-1 - 5) = 6x$			
$4(9 - 2x) - 2x = 8 - 10x$			

1 What is the value of n in the equation $8n + 9 = -n$?

(A) $-\frac{9}{7}$

(B) -1

(C) 1

(D) $\frac{9}{7}$

2 What value of x is the solution to the equation?

$4(x - 1) = 2(x + 1)$

(A) -3

(B) -1

(C) 1

(D) 3

3 What is the solution to the equation?

$0.5x + 20 = 0.6x$

(A) $x = -200$

(B) $x = -2$

(C) $x = 20$

(D) $x = 200$

4 How do the solutions of the equations $\frac{1}{3}(x - 9) = 2x + 7$ and $\frac{4}{3}(x - 4) = -4x$ compare?

(A) The solutions are equal.

(B) The relationship cannot be determined.

(C) The solution of the equation $\frac{1}{3}(x - 9) = 2x + 7$ is less than the solution of $\frac{4}{3}(x - 4) = -4x$.

(D) The solution of the equation $\frac{1}{3}(x - 9) = 2x + 7$ is greater than the solution of $\frac{4}{3}(x - 4) = -4x$.

5 A rectangle has length $\frac{1}{2}x + 5$ and width $\frac{1}{4}x + 4$. If the perimeter of the rectangle is 42 meters, what are the length and the width of the rectangle?

(A) Length: 8 meters; width: 13 meters

(B) Length: 13 meters; width: 8 meters

(C) Length: 15 meters; width: 27 meters

(D) Length: 27 meters; width: 15 meters

6 Which equations have a positive solution?

Select **all** the equations with a positive solution.

(A) $\frac{1}{2}x + 5 = \frac{1}{2}(2 - x)$

(B) $\frac{2}{5}(x + 5) = \frac{1}{5}(x + 4)$

(C) $\frac{3}{2}(x - 8) = \frac{1}{4}x + 3$

(D) $\frac{1}{3}x + 6 = \frac{3}{4}(x + 8)$

(E) $\frac{5}{2}(x - 3) = \frac{5}{3}x - \frac{5}{2}$

7 The area A of a trapezoid is given by $A = \frac{1}{2}h(b_1 + b_2)$, where h is the height and b_1 and b_2 are the lengths of the bases. Suppose the area of a trapezoid is 98 square meters, the height is 7 meters, and the length of one base is 11 meters. What is the length of the other base in meters?

8 A triangle has side lengths of $2x + 1$, $-x + 37$, and $4x - 8$. If the perimeter of the triangle is 125 feet, what is the value of x?

Name _____

9 Ryan and Nate are swimming in a lake. Ryan swims $\frac{5}{4}$ meters per second. Nate swims $\frac{4}{5}$ meter per second. If Nate starts 45 meters ahead of Ryan, how many seconds does it take Ryan to catch Nate?

Plot the answer on the number line.

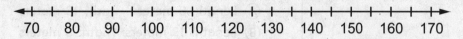

10 The booster club sets up a hot dog stand for fundraising at a middle school. The club receives $12 in donations while members set up the stand. The club sells hot dogs for $1.75. Each hot dog costs the club $0.50, and other supplies cost $57. The club wants to know how many hot dogs they must sell to break even. What is an equation that represents this situation, where h represents the number of hot dogs sold?

_____

11 Solve the equation for y.

$27.3 - 4y = 2.5y$

_____

12 What is the value of m in the equation

$12m - 18 = -4m$?

_____

13 Solve the equation $5(d + 7) = 4(d - 8)$.

$d =$ _____

14 Solve the equation $-\frac{3}{5}(x - 10) = \frac{6}{5}x + 2$.

$x =$ _____

1 A system of equations is graphed below.

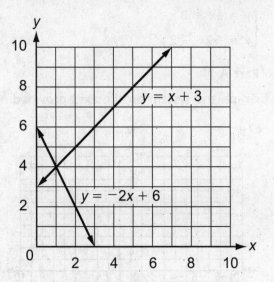

What is the solution of the system?

Ⓐ (0, 3)

Ⓑ (0, 6)

Ⓒ (1, 4)

Ⓓ (4, 1)

2 A system of equations is shown below.

$$\begin{cases} y = -2x + 1 \\ y = -\frac{3}{5}x \end{cases}$$

Does the ordered pair (−5, 3) satisfy the system, and for what reason?

Ⓐ Yes, because it satisfies both equations of the system.

Ⓑ No, because it satisfies only the equation $y = -2x - 1$.

Ⓒ No, because it satisfies only the equation $y = -\frac{3}{5}x$.

Ⓓ No, because it satisfies neither equation of the system.

3 A system of equations is graphed below.

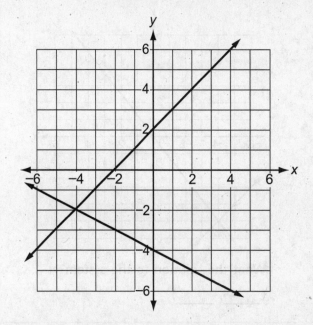

Which ordered pair is the solution of the system?

Ⓐ (−4, −2)

Ⓑ (−4, 2)

Ⓒ (−2, −4)

Ⓓ (2, 4)

4 For which system of equations is the ordered pair (−8, 4) a solution?

Select the **two** correct answers.

Ⓐ $\begin{cases} y = -\frac{3}{4}x + 2 \\ y = \frac{3}{4}x - 10 \end{cases}$

Ⓓ $\begin{cases} y = \frac{3}{5}x + \frac{44}{5} \\ y = \frac{6}{5}x + \frac{68}{5} \end{cases}$

Ⓑ $\begin{cases} y = -\frac{2}{3}x - \frac{4}{3} \\ y = -\frac{7}{4}x - 10 \end{cases}$

Ⓔ $\begin{cases} y = -\frac{3}{8}x + 7 \\ y = \frac{1}{9}x + \frac{44}{9} \end{cases}$

Ⓒ $\begin{cases} y = \frac{5}{2}x + 24 \\ y = \frac{6}{7}x + \frac{20}{7} \end{cases}$

5 A system of equations is graphed below.

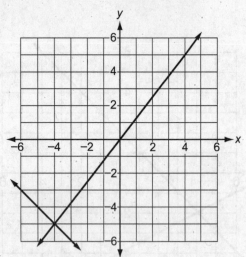

What the solution to the system?

(_____ , _____)

6 Desiree solved the system shown by graphing the equations.

$$\begin{cases} y = 3x - 5 \\ y = -x + 7 \end{cases}$$

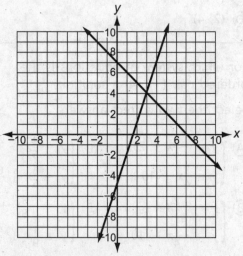

What is the solution to the system?

Ⓐ (0, 7)

Ⓑ (3, 4)

Ⓒ (4, 3)

Ⓓ (7, 0)

7 Consider the following system of equations.

$$\begin{cases} y = \frac{1}{2}x + 3 \\ y = -2x - 2 \end{cases}$$

Part A

Graph the system on the axes provided.

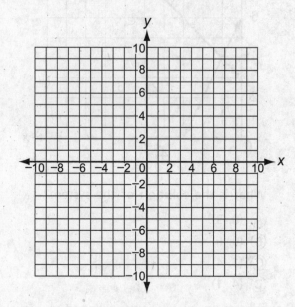

Part B

What is the solution to the system?

(_____ , _____)

8 Place an X in the table to show whether the ordered pair (2, 1) is a solution to each system of equations.

	Yes	No
$\begin{cases} y = 3x - 5 \\ y = \frac{1}{2}x \end{cases}$		
$\begin{cases} y = -4x + 9 \\ y = x + 4 \end{cases}$		
$\begin{cases} y = -\frac{1}{3}x + 6 \\ y = \frac{4}{3}x - 4 \end{cases}$		

1 A system of equations is shown.

$$\begin{cases} 4x + 3y = 4 \\ y = -3x - 2 \end{cases}$$

Which expression can you substitute into the indicated equation to solve the system?

(A) $-3x - 2$ for x in $4x + 3y = 4$

(B) $-3x - 2$ for y in $4x + 3y = 4$

(C) $4x + 3y$ for x in $y = -3x - 2$

(D) $4x + 3y$ for y in $y = -3x - 2$

2 A system of equations is shown.

$$\begin{cases} -4x + y = -1 \\ 2x + 2y = -2 \end{cases}$$

What is the solution to the system?

(A) $(1, 3)$

(B) $(-2, 1)$

(C) $(0, -1)$

(D) $(-1, 0)$

3 A system of equations is shown.

$$\begin{cases} 2x + y = 3 \\ -4x - 2y = -6 \end{cases}$$

Which of the following BEST describes the number of solutions to the system?

(A) no solutions

(B) one solution

(C) two solutions

(D) infinitely many solutions

4 A system of equations is shown.

$$\begin{cases} y = 3x - 6 \\ y = 2x \end{cases}$$

What is the solution of the system?

(A) $(6, 12)$

(B) $(12, 6)$

(C) $(3, 3)$

(D) $(3, 6)$

5 Place an X in the table to show the number of solutions for each system of equations.

	Infinitely Many Solutions	One Solution	No Solutions
$\begin{cases} -14x - 20y = 42 \\ -7x - 10y = 21 \end{cases}$			
$\begin{cases} x + y = 5 \\ -2x - 2y = 10 \end{cases}$			
$\begin{cases} x + y = 6 \\ x + 2y = 6 \end{cases}$			
$\begin{cases} -x - y = -14 \\ -x - y = 14 \end{cases}$			

6 A system of equations is shown.

$$\begin{cases} y = 3x + 20 \\ y = 5x + 2 \end{cases}$$

What is the solution to the system?

Ⓐ (9, 47)

Ⓑ (9, 27)

Ⓒ (−9, −7)

Ⓓ (−9, −43)

---

7 Graph the system of equations in order to estimate the solution.

$$\begin{cases} y = \frac{8}{3}x - 10 \\ y = -\frac{1}{3}x - 1 \end{cases}$$

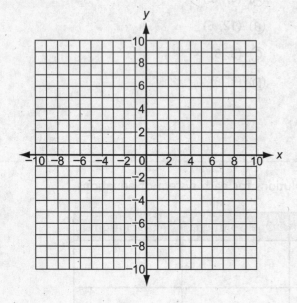

8 Solve the following system of equations algebraically.

$$\begin{cases} -x + y = 4 \\ 5x + 2y = 1 \end{cases}$$

What are the coordinates of the solution?

(_____ , _____)

---

9 Consider the following system of equations.

$$\begin{cases} -2x + 4y = 5 \\ -2x + 4y = 6 \end{cases}$$

Fill in the blanks with words or phrases from the list to correctly complete the sentence.

The system has _____ because substitution results in a statement that will _____ be true.

| always | infinitely many solutions | never |
| no solutions | one solution | sometimes |

---

10 The cost, c, in dollars of a taxi ride is related to the distance, d, in miles of the ride. The cost for taxi A is given by the equation $c = 3.5d + 2$, and the cost for taxi B is given by $c = 3d + 5$.

The distance for which each taxi ride costs the same is _____ miles. A trip of this distance would cost $ _____ .

1 Which pair of points forms a line that does not intersect the line passing through the points (5, 7) and (7, 7)?

Ⓐ (−4, −5) and (−1, −2)

Ⓑ (−5, 3) and (−5, 8)

Ⓒ (−2, −2) and (3, 3)

Ⓓ (8, −9) and (11, −9)

2 Skylar is buying watermelon and pineapple for a fruit salad. Watermelon costs $0.59 per pound, and pineapple costs $2.29 per pound. Skylar buys 7 pounds of fruit and spends $9.23. How much does Skylar spend just on pineapple?

Ⓐ $2.36   Ⓒ $4.00

Ⓑ $3.00   Ⓓ $6.87

3 At what point does the line that passes through the points (−5, −6) and (−3, 2) intersect with the line with equation $y = x - 4$?

Ⓐ (−5, −6)   Ⓒ (−1, 10)

Ⓑ (2, −2)   Ⓓ (−6, −10)

4 There are 25 coins inside a container. Some of the coins are nickels, and the rest are quarters. The value of the coins is $4.05. Let n represent the number of nickels, and let q represent the number of quarters. Which system of equations represents this situation?

Ⓐ $\begin{cases} n + q = 4.05 \\ 5n + 25q = 25 \end{cases}$

Ⓑ $\begin{cases} n + q = 4.05 \\ 0.5n + 0.25q = 25 \end{cases}$

Ⓒ $\begin{cases} n + q = 25 \\ 0.05n + 0.25q = 4.05 \end{cases}$

Ⓓ $\begin{cases} n + q = 25 \\ 5n + 25q = 4.05 \end{cases}$

5 Rosa buys keychains and refrigerator magnets as souvenirs for family and friends. Keychains cost $2 each, and refrigerator magnets cost $1 each. Let x represent the number of keychains that Rosa bought, and let y represent the number of refrigerator magnets.

Place an X in the table to match each situation with the correct system of equations.

	$\begin{cases} -x + y = 12 \\ 2x + y = 18 \end{cases}$	$\begin{cases} x + y = 12 \\ 2x + y = 18 \end{cases}$	$\begin{cases} x + y = 12 \\ 2x - y = 18 \end{cases}$
Rosa bought 12 items and paid a total of $18.			
Rosa bought 12 more refrigerator magnets than keychains and paid a total of $18.			
Rosa bought 12 items and paid $18 more for the keychains than for the refrigerator magnets.			

6 Jesse sells skis and snowboards at a sporting goods store. The store earns a profit of $52 for each pair of skis sold and a profit of $64 for each snowboard sold. If Jesse's store sold a total of 83 pairs of skis and snowboards and earned a profit of $4,892 in November, how many pairs of skis and how many snowboards did the store sell that month?

Jesse sold _____ pairs of skis and _____ snowboards.

7 Two containers are being filled with water. One begins with 8 gallons of water and is filled at a rate of 3.5 gallons per minute. The other begins with 24 gallons and is filled at 3.25 gallons per minute. How long will it take for both of the containers to have the same amount of water? How much water will be in each container?

It will take _____ minutes for both

containers to have _____ gallons of water.

8 A movie theater charges $12.00 for adults and $4.50 for children under the age of ten. A group of adults and children went to the movies and spent $75 on 10 tickets. How many adults and how many children went to the movie?

Adults: _____

Children: _____

9 A high school band sold mums and poinsettias for a fundraiser. Each mum costs $8.00. Each poinsettia costs $3.00.

The band sold a total of 128 mums and poinsettias and earned $659.00.

Fill in the blanks to complete the sentence.

The band sold _____ mums and

_____ poinsettias.

10 Angeline earns $58.50 selling lemonade over the weekend. She sold x small cups for $1.50 each and y large cups for $3 each. She sold a total of 27 cups. How many small and large cups of lemonade did she sell?

Fill in the blanks to complete the sentence.

Angeline sold _____ small cups and _____ large cups.

1 A graph that relates *y* to *x* is shown.

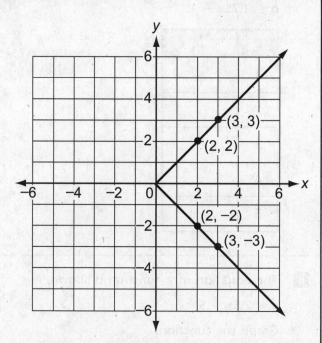

Which is the BEST description of the relation shown?

Ⓐ It is not a function because both (2, 2) and (2, −2) have the same *x*-coordinate.

Ⓑ It is a function because both (2, 2) and (2, −2) have the same *x*-coordinate.

Ⓒ It is not a function because for each *x*-coordinate, there is exactly one *y*-coordinate.

Ⓓ It is a function because for each *x*-coordinate, there is exactly one *y*-coordinate.

2 Which BEST describes a function?

Ⓐ It assigns to each input no outputs.

Ⓑ It assigns to each input exactly one output.

Ⓒ It assigns to each input one or more outputs.

Ⓓ It assigns to each input more than one output.

3 The table below shows some inputs and the corresponding outputs.

Input	Output
−2	4
−1	2
0	0
1	−2
2	−4

Does the table represent a function? Why or why not?

Ⓐ Yes, because the inputs and outputs are integers.

Ⓑ Yes, because each input has exactly one output assigned to it.

Ⓒ No, because there are inputs that have more than one output assigned to them.

Ⓓ No, because there are positive inputs that have negative outputs, and there are negative inputs that have positive outputs.

4 Which of the following sets of ordered pairs (*x*, *y*) represent *y* as a function of *x*?

Select **all** the correct answers.

Ⓐ {(1, 2), (1, 3), (1, 4), (1, 5)}

Ⓑ {(2.5, 8), (3.5, 8), (2.5, 2), (4.5, 2)}

Ⓒ {(−1, 1), (0, 0), (1, 1), (2, 2)}

Ⓓ {(−5, −7.0), (−4, −5.6), (−3, −4.2), (−2, −2.8)}

Ⓔ {(4, −2), (1, −1), (0, 0), (4, 2)}

Ⓕ $\left\{ \left(\frac{1}{2}, 0 \right), \left(1, \frac{1}{2} \right), \left(\frac{3}{2}, 1 \right), \left(2, \frac{3}{2} \right) \right\}$

5 A horizontal line and a vertical line are shown.

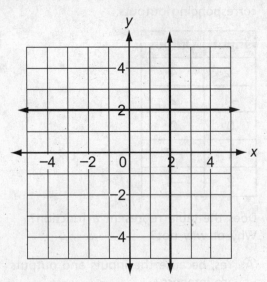

Which line represents a function, and why?

Ⓐ the vertical line, because for every *y*-value there is one and only one *x*-value

Ⓑ the vertical line, because for every *x*-value there is one and only one *y*-value

Ⓒ the horizontal line, because for every *y*-value there is one and only one *x*-value

Ⓓ the horizontal line, because for every *x*-value there is one and only one *y*-value

6 The table below represents a function.

x	y
−6	9
−4	6
−2	3
0	0
2	−3
4	−6

What could be the equation of the function?

Ⓐ $y = -\frac{1}{2}x$

Ⓑ $y = \frac{1}{2}x$

Ⓒ $y = -1.5x$

Ⓓ $y = 1.5x$

7 Complete the table using the function $b = 1.75a + 1$.

a	b
1	
2	
3	
4	
5	

8 The equation of a function is shown.

$y = 2.5x + 5$

Graph the function.

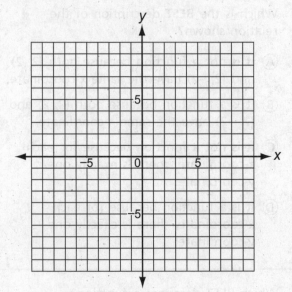

1 The graph of a line is shown.

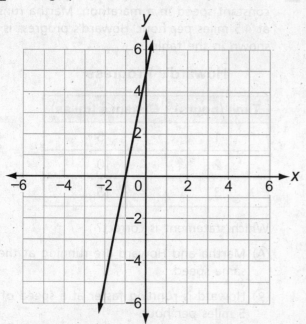

Which function's graph has the same
x-intercept as the line?

(A) $y = -5x - 5$

(B) $y = -5x + 5$

(C) $y = 5x - 1$

(D) $y = \frac{1}{5}x - 1$

2 Raymond and Jose are traveling at a constant
speed in a race. Raymond travels at 5 miles
per hour. Jose's progress is shown in the table.

Jose's Progress

Time (hours)	Distance (miles)
1	5.25
2	10.5
3	15.75

After 5 hours, how much further in miles is
the faster racer than the slower racer?

3 The rate of change for linear function A
is $\frac{1}{3}$. Its graph has a *y*-intercept of 1.
The graph below represents function B.

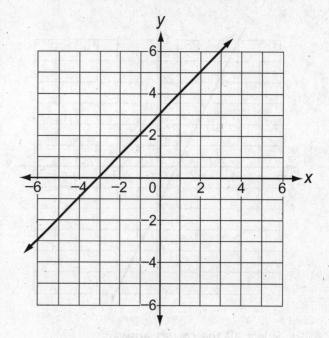

What do the graphs of these two functions
have in common?

(A) the point (1, 4)

(B) the *y*-intercept

(C) the slope

(D) the *x*-intercept

4 The graph of a linear function passes
through the points whose coordinates are
given in the table shown.

x	0	1	2	3
y	−0.5	−0.25	0	0.25

The graph of which function has the same
slope as the graph of the function
represented in the table?

(A) $y = -0.25x - 2$

(B) $y = 0.25x + 5$

(C) $y = 4x - 5$

(D) $y = -4x + 3$

5 Which functions have graphs that share the x-intercept, y-intercept, or slope with the graph of the function shown?

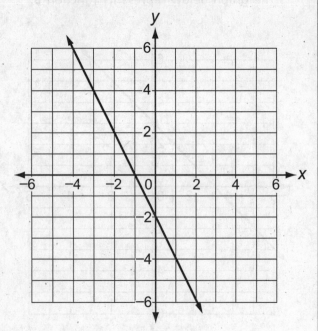

Select **all** the correct answers.

Ⓐ $y = 2x - 2$

Ⓑ $y = -\frac{1}{2}x + 2$

Ⓒ $y = 2x + 2$

Ⓓ $y = -2x + 2$

Ⓔ $y = \frac{1}{2}x + 2$

Ⓕ $y = \frac{1}{2}x - 2$

6 Eli and Alayna are hiking separately on the same 6-mile mountain trail. Eli has already hiked up the mountain from the base and is now hiking back down at a rate of 1.65 miles per hour. Alayna starts hiking up the trail from the base at the same time Eli starts hiking down. The function $d = 1.35t$, where d is distance in miles and t is time in hours, gives Alayna's distance from the start of the trail on her way up the mountain. At what point on the trail do Eli and Alayna meet?

_____ miles from the base

7 Martha and Howard are running at a constant speed in a marathon. Martha runs at 4.5 miles per hour. Howard's progress is shown in the table.

Howard's Progress

Time (hours)	Distance (miles)
1	5
2	10
3	15

Which statement is correct?

Ⓐ Martha and Howard are running at the same speed.

Ⓑ Howard is running faster at a speed of 5 miles per hour.

Ⓒ Martha is running faster at a speed of 4.5 miles per hour.

Ⓓ Howard is running slower at a speed of 4.5 miles per hour.

8 The rate of change for linear function A is −6. Its graph crosses the y-axis at (0, 12). Linear function B is represented by the table shown.

x	0	2	4	6
y	3	9	15	21

What do the graphs of functions A and B have in common?

Ⓐ the y-intercept

Ⓑ the point (1, 6)

Ⓒ the x-intercept

Ⓓ the slope

1 Which equation does not represent a
linear function?

Ⓐ $y = x$

Ⓑ $y = 9$

Ⓒ $y = x + 2$

Ⓓ $y = x^2 + 9$

2 In the right triangle shown, the equation
for the hypotenuse is $y = \frac{4}{5}x + 1$, the
equation for the longer leg is $y = -3$, and
the equation for the shorter leg is $x = 5$.

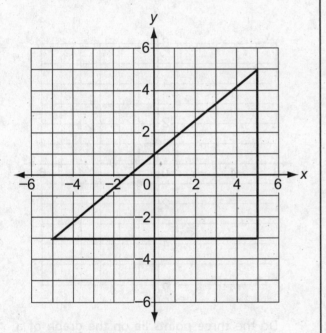

Which statement is correct?

Ⓐ Each of the equations represents a
linear function.

Ⓑ The equation for the longer leg
does not represent a linear function.

Ⓒ The equation for the shorter leg
does not represent a linear function.

Ⓓ The equation for the hypotenuse
does not represent a linear function.

3 Which points are on the graph of a
linear function?

Ⓐ (1, 1), (1, 3), and (1, 6)

Ⓑ (0, 0), (1, 1), and (2, 4)

Ⓒ (−1, 2), (0, 3), and (1, 2)

Ⓓ (−2, 11), (−1, 9), and (0, 7)

4 Which equations represent a function that
is not linear?

Select **all** the correct answers.

Ⓐ $y = 3x + 12$

Ⓑ $y = -6x + x^2$

Ⓒ $y = x^2 + 2$

Ⓓ $y = 10x$

Ⓔ $y = x^3$

Ⓕ $y = 9$

5 A table of values is shown.

x	1	2	3	4	5	6
y	3	6	11	18	27	38

Do the ordered pairs in the table represent
a linear function?

Ⓐ Yes, they represent the linear function
$y = x^2 + 2$.

Ⓑ Yes, they represent the linear function
$y = 3x$.

Ⓒ Yes, they represent the function $4x - 1$.

Ⓓ No, they do not represent a linear
function.

Name _____

6 Place an X in the table to show whether or not each equation represents a linear function.

	Linear Function	Not a Linear Function
$y = 5x$		
$y = 2x^2 - 6$		
$y = -3x + 12$		
$x + 7y = 21$		
$xy = 13$		
$x = -3$		

7 Bella pays to rent a boat. The cost is $22.50 per hour plus a base fee of $14. What is an equation that represents the total amount in dollars Bella pays, t, for h hours?

_____

8 Write the equation $y + 4 = \frac{3}{5}(x - 15)$ in slope-intercept form.

_____

9 Write $x = 11y - 2$ in slope-intercept form.

_____

10 Vladimir is walking down the street at a speed of 4 miles per hour. Write an equation for the distance in miles, d, that Vladimir walks over time in hours, t.

_____

11 Write $6x - 2y = 0$ in slope-intercept form.

_____

12 Three points are plotted as shown.

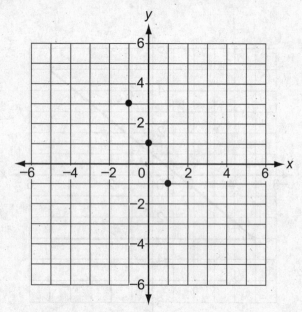

Do the three points lie on the graph of a linear function? If so, what is the equation of the function?

Ⓐ No, the points do not lie on the graph of a linear function.

Ⓑ Yes, the points lie on the graph of the linear function $y = 2x + 1$.

Ⓒ Yes, the points lie on the graph of the linear function $y = -2x + 1$.

Ⓓ Yes, the points lie on the graph of the linear function $y = -2x - 1$.

1 A table of values is shown.

x	0	1	2	3
y	2	4	6	8

What is the rate of change for the relationship described by the data in the table?

Ⓐ −2

Ⓑ −$\frac{1}{2}$

Ⓒ $\frac{1}{2}$

Ⓓ 2

2 A table of values is shown.

x	3	4	5	6
y	9	12	15	18

Which equation shows the relationship in the table?

Ⓐ $y = \frac{1}{4}x$

Ⓑ $y = \frac{1}{3}x$

Ⓒ $y = 3x$

Ⓓ $y = 4x$

3 A graph is shown.

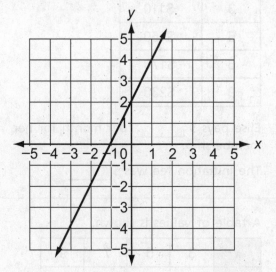

Which of the following is the equation of the line on the graph?

Ⓐ $y = 2x + 2$

Ⓑ $y = 2x − 2$

Ⓒ $y = -2x + 2$

Ⓓ $y = -2x − 2$

4 The table shows the amount of gas used by a household over time.

Household Gas Use

Number of Weeks	2	3	4	5	6
Gas Used (ft³)	80	120	160	200	240

What is the rate of change in cubic feet of gas per week for the data in the table?

Ⓐ −160

Ⓑ −40

Ⓒ 40

Ⓓ 160

5 Vincent's savings over several weeks are shown in the table.

Vincent's Savings

Time (weeks)	2	4	6	8	10
Savings (dollars)	75	115	155	195	235

If a linear function models Vincent's savings over time, how much money did he initially have?

Ⓐ $0

Ⓑ $35

Ⓒ $40

Ⓓ $75

6 The table shows a hot air balloon's height, h, in feet during a descent at various times in seconds, t.

Hot Air Balloon Height

Time (seconds)	Height (feet)
5	1,150
10	1,090
15	1,030
20	970
25	910

What is the rate of change?

_____ feet per second

7 Place an X in the table to match each description of Sue's activity with the function modeling Sue's elevation, e, in feet at time in minutes, t.

	$e = -20t + 100$	$e = 20t - 100$	$e = 20t + 100$
While hiking on a hill, Sue starts at an elevation of 100 feet and ascends at a rate of 20 feet per minute.			
While scuba diving, Sue starts at an elevation of 100 feet below sea level and ascends at a rate of 20 feet per minute.			
While hiking on a hill, Sue starts at an elevation of 100 feet and descends at a rate of 20 feet per minute.			

8 The table shows the relationship between two variables.

x	2	4	6	8	10
y	13	19	25	31	37

What are the rate of change and initial value of the function?

The rate of change is _____.

The initial value is _____.

9 The graph shows the relationship between two variables.

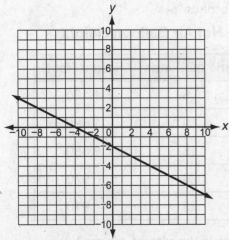

What equation represents the relationship shown in the graph?

10 Elise recently joined a gym. She paid an initiation fee when she joined, and now pays a fee each month. The table shows the total that Elise had paid at the end of several months.

Elise's Gym Membership

Month	Total Paid
3	$110
5	$150
6	$170
9	$230

Elise pays $ _____ per month for her membership.

The initiation fee was $ _____.

11 A table of values is shown.

x	3	5	7	9
y	7.5	12.5	17.5	22.5

What equation shows the relationship shown in the table?

1 Which of the following graphs does not show a linear relationship?

Ⓐ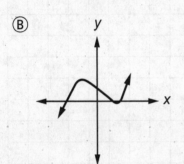

Ⓑ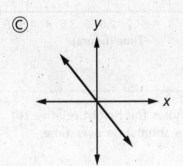

Ⓒ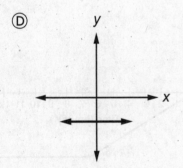

Ⓓ

2 The graph of a function is shown.

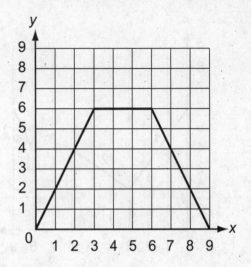

In the graph, for what values of x is y increasing?

Ⓐ between $x = 0$ and $x = 3$

Ⓑ between $x = 3$ and $x = 6$

Ⓒ between $x = 6$ and $x = 9$

Ⓓ The function is never increasing.

3 The graph of a function is shown.

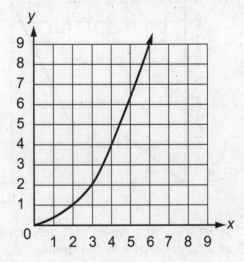

What words best describe the function?

Ⓐ increasing and linear

Ⓑ increasing and nonlinear

Ⓒ decreasing and linear

Ⓓ decreasing and nonlinear

4 The graph of a function is shown.

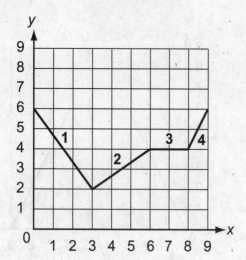

What segment of the graph shows the function having a constant value?

(A) segment 1   (C) segment 3

(B) segment 2   (D) segment 4

5 The graph of a function is shown.

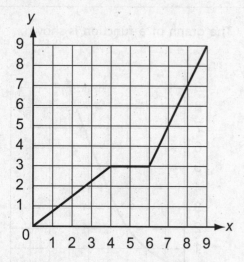

Select **all** of the words that describe y as a function of x in the graph.

(A) always increasing

(B) always decreasing

(C) constant between $x = 4$ and $x = 6$

(D) constant between $x = 0$ and $x = 4$

(E) increasing between $x = 0$ and $x = 4$

(F) decreasing between $x = 6$ and $x = 9$

6 An airplane takes off and climbs to its cruising altitude at a constant rate, taking 30 minutes to reach 36,000 feet. Once the airplane reaches its cruising altitude, it flies at that altitude for 3 hours. It then descends at a constant rate for 30 minutes until landing. Graph the airplane's altitude a as a function of time t.

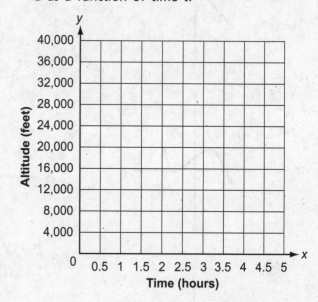

7 The graph shows the height relative to sea level of a submarine over time.

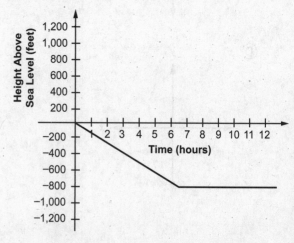

Fill in the blank to complete the sentence.

After descending at a constant rate, the submarine maintains a depth of _____ feet.

1 Under which transformation is the orientation of a line segment not preserved?

Ⓐ reflection

Ⓑ rotation

Ⓒ translation

Ⓓ dilation

2 A 6-inch line segment undergoes a rotation of 180° about a point. How long is the resulting line segment?

_____ in.

3 Consider line segments $\overline{AB}$, $\overline{CD}$, and $\overline{EF}$.

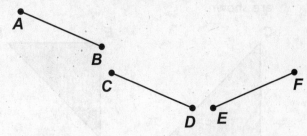

Fill in the blanks with words from the list to correctly complete the sentences.

$\overline{CD}$ is produced by _____ $\overline{AB}$.

$\overline{EF}$ is produced by _____ $\overline{CD}$.

| translating | reflecting | rotating |

4 Place an X in the table to show whether or not each diagram shows a translation.

	Translation	Not a Translation
(diagram A, B, C, D)		
(diagram A, B, C, D)		
(diagram A, B, C, D)		

Name _____

5 Triangle *ABC* and its transformation *DEF* are shown.

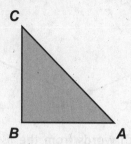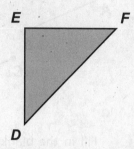

What transformation of triangle *ABC* produced triangle *DEF*?

Ⓐ horizontal translation

Ⓑ rotation about point *A*

Ⓒ reflection across a vertical line

Ⓓ dilation about point *B*

6 A 22-centimeter line segment is translated 12 centimeters to the right. How long is the resulting line segment?

_____ cm

7 One line segment was rotated to produce another line segment. Which statement is correct about the two line segments?

Ⓐ They have the same length but not the same orientation.

Ⓑ They have the same orientation but not the same length.

Ⓒ They have both the same length and the same orientation.

Ⓓ They have neither the same length nor the same orientation.

8 The following image shows two line segments.

Which transformation is represented by the image?

Ⓐ flip

Ⓑ reflection

Ⓒ rotation

Ⓓ translation

9 The following image shows two line segments.

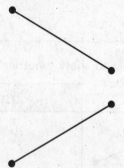

Which transformation is represented by the image?

Ⓐ reflection

Ⓑ rotation

Ⓒ slide

Ⓓ translation

10 Under which of these transformations will the length of a line segment stay the same?

Ⓐ reflection

Ⓑ rotation

Ⓒ translation

Ⓓ The length will stay the same for all of these transformations.

1 In triangle *ABC*, the measure of ∠*A* = 40°, the measure of ∠*B* = 90°, and the measure of ∠*C* = 50°. If the triangle is rotated 90° clockwise about a point, what is the measure of the image of ∠*A*?

(A) 40°

(B) 50°

(C) 90°

(D) 130°

2 Quadrilateral *WXYZ* is the image of quadrilateral *ABCD* translated 9 units left and 4 units up. If the measure of ∠*A* is known, what other angle measure is known?

(A) ∠*W*

(B) ∠*X*

(C) ∠*Y*

(D) ∠*Z*

3 No two angles of triangle *ABC* have the same measure. Triangle *FGH* is the image of triangle *ABC* after being translated 5 units to the right and 8 units down.

Place an X in the table to determine whether the angles have the same measure.

	Same	Different
∠*A* and ∠*H*		
∠*C* and ∠*H*		
∠*B* and ∠*F*		
∠*A* and ∠*F*		

4 Trapezoid *EFGH* is reflected across the *x*-axis and then reflected across the *y*-axis to form trapezoid *ABCD*. What angle of trapezoid *EFGH* must have the same measure as the given angle of trapezoid *ABCD*?

_____ must have the same measure as ∠*B*.

_____ must have the same measure as ∠*C*.

5 Patricia is painting sailboats on her wall using stencils. She uses a stencil of a right triangle for the sail. Patricia paints one sail on the wall, triangle *ABC*, where the measure of ∠*A* = 52°, the measure of ∠*B* = 90°, and the measure of ∠*C* = 38°. She then moves the stencil 8 inches to the right. If she paints a second sail in that spot, triangle *DEF*, what will the measures of the angles be?

the measure of ∠*D* = _____ °

the measure of ∠*E* = _____ °

the measure of ∠*F* = _____ °

6 The image of triangle *ABC* is triangle *ABD* after a reflection across line segment *AB*.

Fill in the blanks with the correct answers from the list to complete the sentences.

Triangle *DAC* must be a(n) _____ triangle.

∠*D* is _____ ∠*C*.

equilateral	isosceles	right
congruent to	larger than	smaller than

7 Triangle *MNO* is the image of triangle *ABC* after a reflection across line *EF*. Which statements must be true?

Select **all** the true statements.

(A) the measure of ∠*M* = the measure of ∠*A*

(B) the measure of ∠*M* = the measure of ∠*C*

(C) the measure of ∠*N* = the measure of ∠*A*

(D) the measure of ∠*N* = the measure of ∠*B*

(E) the measure of ∠*O* = the measure of ∠*C*

8 In quadrilateral *ABCD*, the measure of ∠*A* = 90°, the measure of ∠*B* = 125°, the measure of ∠*C* = 100°, and the measure of ∠*D* = 45°. If quadrilateral *HJKL* is the image of *ABCD* after a translation and a rotation, what is the measure of ∠*L*?

(A) 45°

(B) 90°

(C) 100°

(D) 125°

9 Triangle *MNP* is reflected across a line outside the triangle.

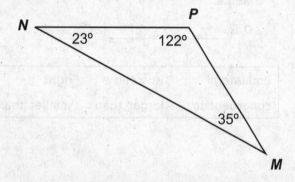

What is the measure in degrees of the image of angle *P*?

10 In triangle *XYZ*, the measure of ∠*X* = 37°, and the measure of ∠*Y* = 88°. If triangle *RST* is the image of triangle *XYZ* after a translation of 8 inches and a rotation of 90° counterclockwise, what is the measure of ∠*T*?

(A) 37°

(B) 55°

(C) 88°

(D) 90°

11 In quadrilateral *FGHJ*, ∠*H* is a right angle. If quadrilateral *CDEF* is the image of *FGHJ* after a reflection, which angle must be a right angle?

(A) ∠*C*

(B) ∠*D*

(C) ∠*E*

(D) ∠*F*

12 Parallelogram *RSTV* is rotated 18° clockwise about point *V*.

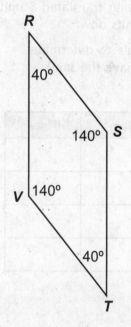

What is the measure in degrees of the image of angle *V*?

© Houghton Mifflin Harcourt Publishing Company

1 A regular octagon is rotated 5°
counterclockwise about a point in
the interior of the figure. How many pairs
of sides are parallel in the image?

Ⓐ 1

Ⓑ 3

Ⓒ 4

Ⓓ 5

2 The image of pentagon *ABCDE* after it is
translated right 8 units and up 3 units is
pentagon *QRSTU*. If sides $\overline{BC}$ and $\overline{AE}$ are
parallel in *ABCDE* and there are no other
parallel sides, which sides in the image
are parallel?

Ⓐ $\overline{RS}$ and $\overline{QU}$

Ⓑ $\overline{QR}$ and $\overline{ST}$

Ⓒ $\overline{RS}$ and $\overline{TU}$

Ⓓ $\overline{ST}$ and $\overline{QU}$

3 Quadrilateral *WXYZ* is the image of
quadrilateral *ABCD* after it is rotated 90°
clockwise about a point exterior to the
figure and then translated left
3 centimeters. If sides $\overline{WZ}$ and $\overline{XY}$ are
parallel in quadrilateral *WXYZ*, which
sides must be parallel in the original
quadrilateral?

Ⓐ $\overline{AB}$ and $\overline{AD}$

Ⓑ $\overline{BC}$ and $\overline{AD}$

Ⓒ $\overline{CD}$ and $\overline{BC}$

Ⓓ $\overline{AB}$ and $\overline{BC}$

4 Rectangle *ABCD* is translated 4 millimeters
down. Which sides of the image are parallel
after the translation?

Ⓐ the images of $\overline{AB}$ and $\overline{BC}$

Ⓑ the images of $\overline{BC}$ and $\overline{CD}$

Ⓒ the images of $\overline{AB}$ and $\overline{CD}$

Ⓓ the images of $\overline{AD}$ and $\overline{CD}$

Ⓔ the images of $\overline{AB}$ and $\overline{AD}$

Ⓕ the images of $\overline{AD}$ and $\overline{BC}$

5 Trapezoid *KLMN* is the image of trapezoid
PQRS after a reflection. Side *QR* of trapezoid
PQRS is not one of the trapezoid's bases.
Which side is parallel to $\overline{KL}$?

$\overline{KL}$ || _____

6 In pentagon *VWXYZ*, $\overline{VW}$ || $\overline{YZ}$ and $\overline{XY}$ || $\overline{VZ}$.

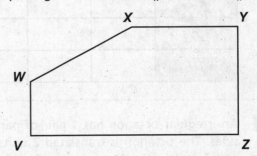

Pentagon *DEFGH* is the image of pentagon
VWXYZ after a reflection across a line
outside of the figure and a rotation about
one of the vertices. Which sides are parallel
to the given sides?

$\overline{DE}$ || _____

$\overline{FG}$ || _____

7 Regular hexagon *EFGHIJ* is transformed with a rotation and a reflection to form hexagon *PQRSTU*.

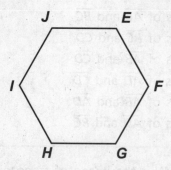

Which sides of hexagon *PQRSTU* are parallel?

Place an X in the table to indicate which pairs of sides in *PQRSTU* are parallel.

	$\overline{PU}$	$\overline{ST}$	$\overline{QR}$
$\overline{PQ}$			
$\overline{RS}$			
$\overline{TU}$			

8 An irregular octagon has 1 pair of parallel sides. The octagon is translated 2 units up and 3 units right. How many pairs of parallel sides does the octagon's image have?

Ⓐ 1

Ⓑ 2

Ⓒ 3

Ⓓ 4

9 Parallelogram *MNTP* is rotated 90° clockwise about vertex *N*. How many pairs of parallel sides does the rotated figure have?

_____

10 Quadrilateral *JKLM* has one pair of parallel sides, $\overline{JK}$ and $\overline{LM}$. Quadrilateral *FGHJ* is the image of *JKLM* after a translation and a rotation.

Which pair of sides in *FGHJ* is parallel?

Ⓐ $\overline{FG}$ and $\overline{HJ}$

Ⓑ $\overline{FG}$ and $\overline{GH}$

Ⓒ $\overline{GH}$ and $\overline{HJ}$

Ⓓ $\overline{GH}$ and $\overline{FJ}$

11 An irregular 12-sided polygon has 3 pairs of parallel sides. If the polygon is translated 2 inches to the left and 5 inches down, how many pairs of parallel sides will the image have?

_____

12 Square *WXYZ* is reflected across two lines that are perpendicular to each other.

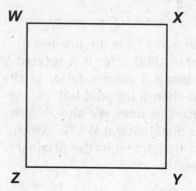

How many pairs of parallel sides does the image have?

_____

1 An equilateral triangle has side lengths of 12 centimeters. The triangle undergoes a translation 4 centimeters to the right and a rotation around one of its vertices. What is the perimeter of the image?

Ⓐ 12 cm

Ⓑ 36 cm

Ⓒ 48 cm

Ⓓ 72 cm

2 Rectangle *ABCD* is 10 inches wide and 18 inches long. The rectangle is reflected across a line exterior to the rectangle, and then rotated around its center. What is the area of the image?

Ⓐ 8 in.^{2}

Ⓑ 28 in.^{2}

Ⓒ 56 in.^{2}

Ⓓ 180 in.^{2}

3 Squares *ABCD* and *DABC* are congruent.

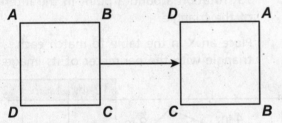

Which series of transformations carries square *ABCD* onto square *DABC*?

Ⓐ a translation to the right and a rotation 90° clockwise around its center

Ⓑ a translation to the left and a reflection across a vertical line

Ⓒ a translation to the right and a rotation 90° counterclockwise around its center

Ⓓ a reflection across a horizontal line and a rotation 90° clockwise around its center

4 The two triangles shown are congruent.

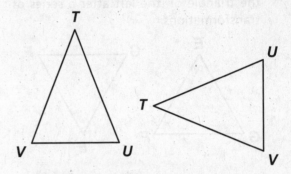

Which series of transformations carry the triangle on the left onto the triangle on the right?

Ⓐ a translation and a rotation 90° clockwise

Ⓑ a translation and a rotation 90° counterclockwise

Ⓒ a reflection across a horizontal line and a rotation 90° clockwise

Ⓓ a reflection across a horizontal line and a rotation 90° counterclockwise

5 The legs of right triangle *XYZ* are 3 feet and 4 feet long, and the hypotenuse is 5 feet long. The triangle undergoes a horizontal reflection and a rotation around vertex *Z*. What is the area of the image?

Ⓐ 6 ft^2

Ⓑ 10 ft^2

Ⓒ 12 ft^2

Ⓓ 60 ft^2

6 The triangle on the right is the image of the triangle on the left after a series of transformations.

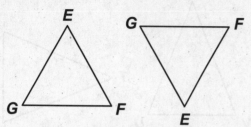

Circle the correct words to complete the sentence.

The triangles are/are not congruent, so

their areas are the same/different and

their perimeters are the same/different.

---

7 Rectangle *WXYZ* has a width of 63 meters and a length of 64 meters. The rectangle undergoes a translation 4 meters to the left and a reflection across a horizontal line.

The perimeter of the image

is _____ meters, and its area

is _____ square meters.

---

8 Consider right triangle *ABC* shown.

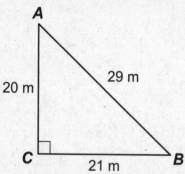

The triangle is rotated 10° counterclockwise around vertex *B* and then translated 1 m to the right.

The perimeter of the image is _____ meters,

and its area is _____ square meters.

9 The pentagon on the right is the image of the pentagon on the left after a series of transformations.

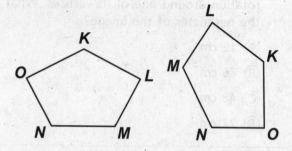

Which two transformations will map pentagon *KLMNO* onto its image?

Select **all** the correct answers.

Ⓐ a rotation

Ⓑ a translation up

Ⓒ a translation down

Ⓓ a reflection across a vertical line

Ⓔ a reflection across a horizontal line

---

10 Each triangle in the table undergoes a reflection across a vertical line and a 75° rotation around a point in the interior of the triangle.

Place an X in the table to match each triangle with the perimeter of its image.

	10 in.	11 in.	12 in.
4 in. / 2 in. / 6 in.			
3 in. / 1 in. / 7 in.			
4 in. / 3 in. / 3 in.			

1 The figure shown is rotated 180° clockwise about the origin.

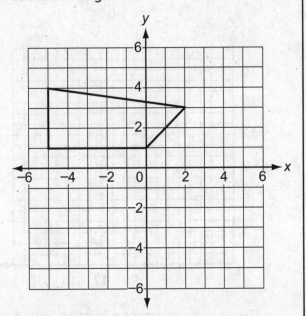

Which ordered pairs are the vertices of the resulting image?

Select **all** the correct ordered pairs.

Ⓐ (−2, −3)

Ⓑ (0, −1)

Ⓒ (1, 5)

Ⓓ (−3, 2)

Ⓔ (5, −4)

Ⓕ (5, −1)

2 The vertices of a triangle are located at the points A(0, 1), B(2, 4), and C(3, 0). The triangle is translated 5 units down to obtain △A′B′C′. What are the coordinates of the vertices of △A′B′C′?

Ⓐ A′(−5, 1), B′(−3, 4), C′(−2, 0)

Ⓑ A′(0, −4), B′(2, −1), C′(3, −5)

Ⓒ A′(0, 6), B′(2, 9), C′(3, 5)

Ⓓ A′(5, 1), B′(7, 4), C′(8, 0)

3 Vince is moving a rectangular picture frame on a wall. The picture frame is 2 feet long and 1 foot tall. If the bottom left corner of the wall is designated (0, 0), then the lower left corner of the frame is located at (3, 5), where the x- and y-coordinates are measured in feet. Vince moves the picture frame 2 feet to the right and 1 foot up. What is the new position of the frame? Plot the new position of the frame.

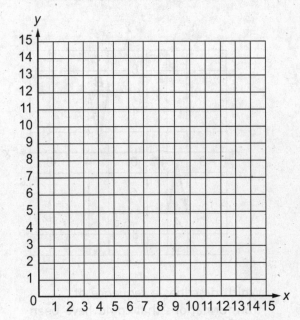

4 A triangle is graphed on a coordinate plane as shown.

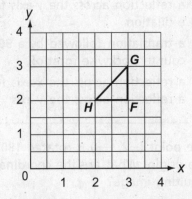

In which quadrant would the triangle be if it were rotated 90° clockwise about the origin?

Ⓐ Quadrant I

Ⓑ Quadrant II

Ⓒ Quadrant III

Ⓓ Quadrant IV

5 A figure graphed on a coordinate plane is reflected across the *y*-axis and then translated 4 units to the left.

Write the correct *x*-coordinate to complete the rule for this transformation.

$(x, y) \longrightarrow ($ _____ $, y)$

6 Ashton applied a sequence of transformations to obtain $\triangle B$ from $\triangle A$ as shown.

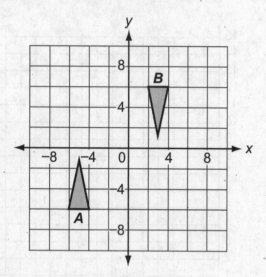

Which describes a sequence of transformations that could have been used?

Ⓐ a translation right followed by a translation up

Ⓑ a reflection across the *y*-axis followed by a dilation

Ⓒ a translation followed by a 90° counterclockwise rotation

Ⓓ a reflection across the *x*-axis followed by a reflection across the *y*-axis

7 The point $(-2, -3)$ is rotated 180° about the origin. What are the coordinates of the resulting image?

Ⓐ $(-2, 3)$

Ⓑ $(2, -3)$

Ⓒ $(2, 3)$

Ⓓ $(3, 2)$

8 Rosa is making a pattern using the square shown, with side length 4 units.

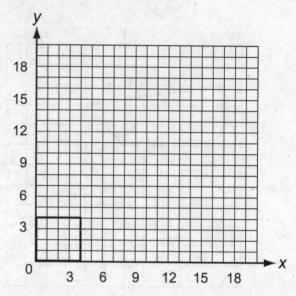

The square undergoes a dilation with a scale factor of $\frac{3}{2}$ centered at the origin, followed by a translation 4 units up and 4 units right.

Plot the image after the transformations.

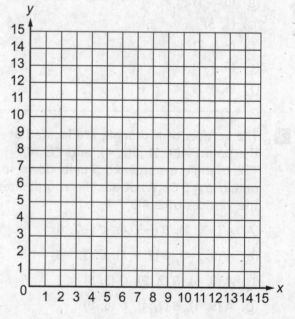

1 A figure is dilated by a scale factor of 3. Which statement about the figure and its image is true?

Ⓐ They are congruent. The perimeters and areas are equal.

Ⓑ They are similar. The perimeter and area of the original figure are tripled.

Ⓒ They are similar. The perimeter of the original figure is multiplied by 3, and the area is multiplied by 9.

Ⓓ They are different shapes and sizes. The perimeter of the original figure is multiplied by 9, and the area is multiplied by 3.

2 Andrew drew $\triangle XYZ$ by dilating $\triangle UVW$. Which statement must be true?

Ⓐ $\triangle UVW$ is congruent to $\triangle XYZ$.

Ⓑ The area of $\triangle XYZ$ is greater than the area of $\triangle UVW$.

Ⓒ The perimeter of $\triangle XYZ$ is less than the perimeter of $\triangle UVW$.

Ⓓ The ratios of corresponding sides of $\triangle XYZ$ and $\triangle UVW$ are equal.

3 Jenya obtained the image of $\triangle ABC$ after a dilation with a scale factor of 3. The area of $\triangle ABC$ is 15 square centimeters, and its perimeter is 20 centimeters. Which statements correctly describe $\triangle ABC$ and its image?

Select **all** the correct statements.

Ⓐ The figures are similar.

Ⓑ The figures are congruent.

Ⓒ The area of the image is 45 cm², and its perimeter is 60 cm.

Ⓓ The area of the image is 15 cm², and its perimeter is 20 cm.

Ⓔ The area of the image is 135 cm², and its perimeter is 60 cm.

Ⓕ The area of the image is 225 cm², and its perimeter is 400 cm.

4 Triangle *MNO* has side lengths of 24 ft, 48 ft, and 32 ft. Which side lengths could belong to a dilation of triangle *MNO*?

Ⓐ 3 ft, 6 ft, 4 ft

Ⓑ 6 ft, 12 ft, 9 ft

Ⓒ 34 ft, 58 ft, 42 ft

Ⓓ 48 ft, 98 ft, 64 ft

5 Rectangle *GHJK* has an area of 121 square inches. Rectangle *NOPQ* is similar to rectangle *GHJK* and has an area of 1 square inch. Which transformation could have been performed on rectangle *GHJK* to obtain rectangle *NOPQ*?

Ⓐ a translation of 11 inches

Ⓑ a translation of 120 inches

Ⓒ a dilation with scale factor of $\frac{1}{11}$

Ⓓ a dilation with scale factor of 11

6 In the figure, $\triangle TUV$ is the image of $\triangle PQR$ after a series of transformations.

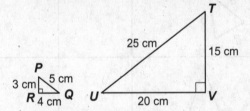

Which sequence maps $\triangle PQR$ onto $\triangle TUV$?

Ⓐ a translation to the right followed by a dilation with a scale factor of $\frac{1}{5}$

Ⓑ a translation to the right followed by a dilation with a scale factor of 5

Ⓒ a reflection across a vertical line followed by a dilation with a scale factor of $\frac{1}{5}$

Ⓓ a reflection across a vertical line followed by a dilation with a scale factor of 5

7 Which figures are similar to the given figure?

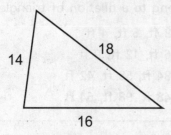

Place an X in the table to show whether each figure is similar or not similar to the given figure.

	Similar	Not Similar
19, 21, 23 triangle		
9, 8, 7 triangle		
18, 16, 14 triangle		

8 Pentagon *RSTUV* is the image of pentagon *JKLMN* after a rotation around a point exterior to pentagon *JKLMN* followed by a dilation with a scale factor of 4. If the area of pentagon *JKLMN* is 120 square centimeters, what is the area of pentagon *RSTUV*?

Ⓐ 16 cm²

Ⓑ 30 cm²

Ⓒ 480 cm²

Ⓓ 1,920 cm²

9 The rectangle shown undergoes a dilation with a scale factor of $\frac{1}{2}$ and a reflection across a vertical line.

8 in. | 20 in. (rectangle)

The area of the rectangle's image is _____ in.², and its perimeter is _____ in.

10 A figure is dilated by a scale factor of 7. Fill in the blanks with the correct answers from the list to complete the sentences.

The image is _____ the original figure. The area of the image is _____ the area of the original figure. The perimeter of the image is _____ the perimeter of the original figure.

similar to	congruent to
a different size and shape than	
7 times	49 times equal to

1 The figure shows two parallel lines intersected by a transversal.

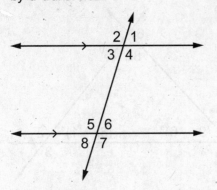

Which is a pair of congruent angles?

Ⓐ ∠1 and ∠2

Ⓑ ∠2 and ∠5

Ⓒ ∠3 and ∠7

Ⓓ ∠5 and ∠8

2 In the figure, △BHE is shown.

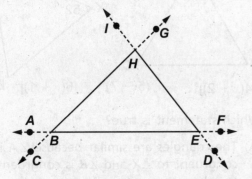

Place an X in the table to show whether each angle is an exterior angle of the triangle.

	Yes	No
∠GHE		
∠ABH		
∠DEB		
∠FED		

3 Which set of angles does not form a triangle?

Ⓐ 76°, 52°, and 52°

Ⓑ 90°, 37°, and 51°

Ⓒ 37°, 65°, and 78°

Ⓓ 120°, 12°, and 48°

4 △ABC and △DEF are similar triangles. If m∠A = 104° and m∠E = 36°, what is m∠C?

Ⓐ 36°

Ⓑ 40°

Ⓒ 76°

Ⓓ 104°

5 In the figure shown, two parallel lines are cut by a transversal.

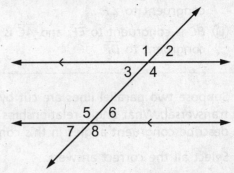

Place an X in the table to show whether each pair is a pair of alternate exterior angles.

	Yes	No
∠7 and ∠4		
∠2 and ∠6		
∠8 and ∠1		
∠2 and ∠7		

6 In the figure, △ABC and △DEF are shown.

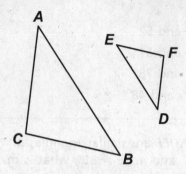

Which of the following guarantees that △ABC and △DEF are similar triangles?

Ⓐ ∠B is congruent to ∠E, and $\overline{BC}$ is congruent to $\overline{EF}$.

Ⓑ ∠C is congruent to ∠F, and $\overline{AC}$ is congruent to $\overline{DF}$.

Ⓒ ∠B is congruent to ∠E, and ∠C is congruent to ∠F.

Ⓓ $\overline{BC}$ is congruent to $\overline{EF}$, and $\overline{AC}$ is congruent to $\overline{DF}$.

7 Suppose two parallel lines are cut by a transversal. What angle relationships always describe congruent angles in this context?

Select **all** the correct answers.

Ⓐ linear pair

Ⓑ corresponding angles

Ⓒ alternate interior angles

Ⓓ alternate exterior angles

Ⓔ same-side interior angles

Ⓕ same-side exterior angles

8 In the triangle, m∠1 = 42° and m∠4 = 81°.

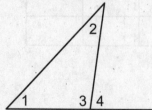

What is m∠2?

Ⓐ 39°   Ⓒ 99°

Ⓑ 57°   Ⓓ 123°

9 The lines shown form a triangle.

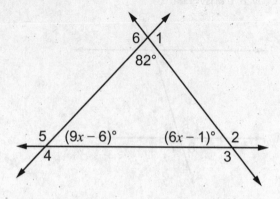

What is the measure in degrees of ∠2?

_____

10 Two triangles are shown.

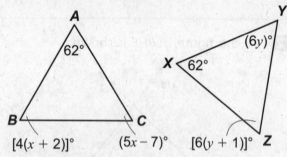

Which statement is true?

Ⓐ The triangles are similar because ∠A is congruent to ∠X and ∠B is congruent to ∠Y.

Ⓑ The triangles are similar because ∠A is congruent to ∠X but ∠B is not congruent to ∠Z.

Ⓒ The triangles are not similar because ∠A is congruent to ∠X and ∠A is congruent to ∠Z.

Ⓓ The triangles are not similar because ∠A is congruent to ∠X but ∠B is not congruent to ∠Y.

1 Three squares are placed to form a right triangle as shown.

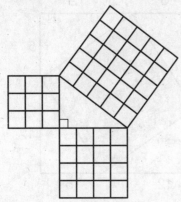

Which statement must be true?

(A) The sum of the areas of the smaller squares is always equal to the area of the largest square.

(B) The sum of the areas of the smaller squares is always greater than the area of the largest square.

(C) The difference of the areas of the smaller squares is always equal to the area of the largest square.

(D) The difference of the areas of the smaller squares is always greater than the area of the largest square.

2 Which expression represents the area of the shaded region in the diagram?

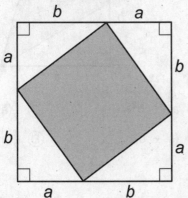

(A) a^2b^2

(B) $a^2 + b^2$

(C) $(a + b)^2$

(D) $(a^2 + b^2)^2$

3 Miriam has two rods that are 7 centimeters and 24 centimeters in length. What length rod will she need to create a right triangle?

(A) 17 centimeters

(B) 21 centimeters

(C) 25 centimeters

(D) 31 centimeters

4 Triangle *RTU* has $UR = 28$, $RT = 45$, and $TU = 53$. What is the measure of angle *R*?

_____

5 Place an X in the table to show whether each set of side lengths can be used to make a right triangle.

	Yes	No
36, 77, 85		
36, 72, 80		
39, 69, 99		
39, 80, 89		

6 A carpenter has boards that are 12 inches, 14 inches, 16 inches, and 20 inches long. Which boards can be used to make a right triangular brace?

The carpenter can use the _____ in.,

_____ in., and _____ in. boards to

make a right triangular brace.

7 The diagram shows the same square divided into a set of triangles and squares in different ways.

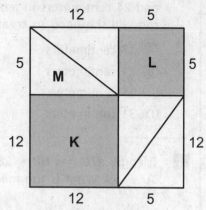
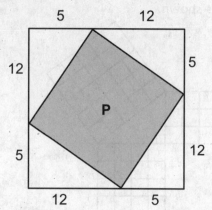

Which statement does the diagram prove?

Ⓐ Four times the area of triangle *M* is equal to the sum of the areas of squares *K* and *L*.

Ⓑ The area of square *K* is equal to the sum of the areas of square *L* and triangle *M*.

Ⓒ The area of square *P* is equal to the sum of the areas of squares *K* and *L*.

Ⓓ Four times the area of triangle *M* is equal to the area of square *P*.

---

8 Triangle *JKL* is formed by three squares with the areas shown in the diagram.

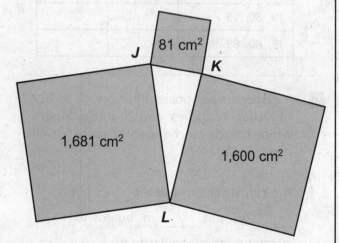

What type of triangle is triangle *JKL*?

Ⓐ acute

Ⓑ equilateral

Ⓒ obtuse

Ⓓ right

9 Which expression represents the area of the shaded region in the diagram?

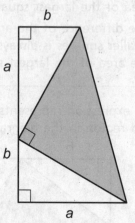

Ⓐ $a^2 + b^2$

Ⓒ $\frac{1}{2}(a + b)^2$

Ⓑ $(a + b)^2$

Ⓓ $\frac{1}{2}(a^2 + b^2)$

1 A diagonal shortcut across a rectangular lot
is 100 feet long. The lot is 60 feet wide.
What is the length of the lot?

Ⓐ 40 ft

Ⓑ 60 ft

Ⓒ 80 ft

Ⓓ 100 ft

2 A triangle is shown.

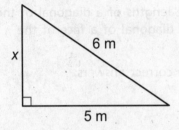

To the nearest tenth of a meter, what is the
unknown side length in the triangle?

Ⓐ 1.0 m

Ⓑ 3.3 m

Ⓒ 7.8 m

Ⓓ 11.0 m

3 The size of a computer screen is measured
along the diagonal. To the nearest inch,
what is the approximate size of a 12 in. by
10.5 in. computer screen?

Ⓐ 6 in.

Ⓑ 16 in.

Ⓒ 23 in.

Ⓓ 34 in.

4 A right rectangular prism is shown.

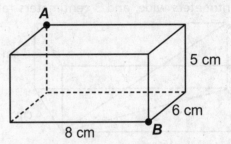

To the nearest centimeter, what is the
approximate length of the diagonal from
point *A* to point *B* in the prism?

Ⓐ 8 cm

Ⓑ 9 cm

Ⓒ 10 cm

Ⓓ 11 cm

5 Consider the triangle shown.

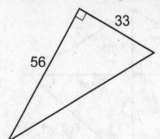

What is the length in units of the
hypotenuse?

_____

6 An isosceles right triangle has legs that are
10 centimeters long. To the nearest tenth of
a centimeter, what is the length of the
hypotenuse?

_____

7 The box shown is 15 centimeters long, 4 centimeters wide, and 3 centimeters tall.

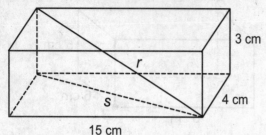

To the nearest tenth of a centimeter, what are the lengths of diagonal *s* and diagonal *r*?

The length of diagonal *s* of the bottom side is _____ centimeters. The length of diagonal *r* of the box is _____ centimeters.

8 Consider the figure shown.

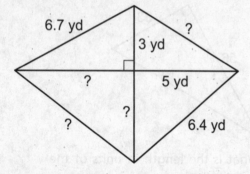

Rounded to the nearest tenth of a yard, what are the unknown lengths in the figure?

Select **all** the correct answers.

Ⓐ 4.0 yd

Ⓑ 5.8 yd

Ⓒ 6.0 yd

Ⓓ 7.2 yd

Ⓔ 7.3 yd

Ⓕ 8.1 yd

9 A right rectangular prism is shown.

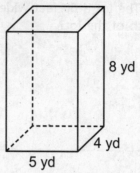

Rounded to the nearest tenth of a yard, what are the lengths of a diagonal of the prism or any diagonal of a face of the prism?

Select **all** the correct answers.

Ⓐ 6.2 yd

Ⓑ 6.4 yd

Ⓒ 8.9 yd

Ⓓ 9.4 yd

Ⓔ 10.2 yd

Ⓕ 12.0 yd

10 Maurice is cleaning out a rain gutter on his house. To get to the gutter, he places a 24 ft ladder against the house so that the top of the ladder reaches the bottom of the gutter. He places the bottom of the ladder so that it is 7 ft from the house. At what height is the bottom of the gutter rounded to the nearest foot?

_____

1 Consider △ABC shown on the coordinate plane.

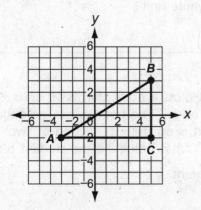

What is the length of $\overline{AB}$ rounded to the nearest unit?

Ⓐ 5   Ⓒ 9

Ⓑ 8   Ⓓ 13

2 Every morning, Cho rides his bicycle from his house to the park and then back to his house. He takes the same route in both directions. His route is shown on the coordinate plane, where each unit represents 1 mile.

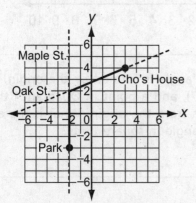

How far does Cho ride every morning rounded to the nearest tenth of a mile?

Ⓐ 5.0 miles   Ⓒ 10.4 miles

Ⓑ 5.4 miles   Ⓓ 20.8 miles

3 To the nearest tenth of a unit, what is the distance between the points (−3, 3) and (1, 2)?

Ⓐ 3.9 units   Ⓒ 5.4 units

Ⓑ 4.1 units   Ⓓ 6.0 units

4 A square is shown on the coordinate plane.

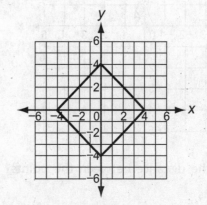

What is the perimeter of the square to the nearest tenth of a unit?

Ⓐ 5.7   Ⓒ 22.6

Ⓑ 16.0   Ⓓ 32.0

5 Points W and X are plotted on a coordinate plane as shown.

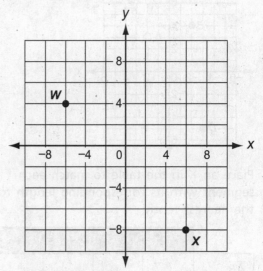

What is the distance between the points to the nearest hundredth of a unit?

6 Points *A* and *B* are plotted on a coordinate plane as shown.

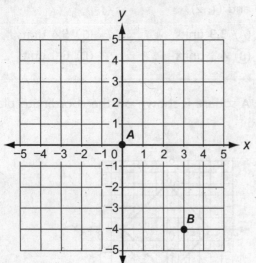

What is the distance between the points?

(A) 3 units

(B) 4 units

(C) 5 units

(D) 7 units

7 Consider the graph shown.

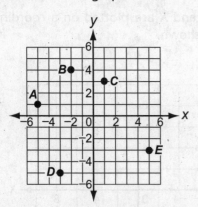

Place an X in the table to match each segment with its corresponding length to the nearest tenth.

	4.2	7.2	8.2	9.9
$\overline{AB}$				
$\overline{CE}$				
$\overline{BE}$				

8 What is the distance between the origin and a point at $(-15, 8)$ rounded to the nearest whole unit?

_____

9 A student plots a point that is 10 units from the origin. The point is not on either axis, but it is on the intersection of two grid lines. What point did the student plot?

Plot the point.

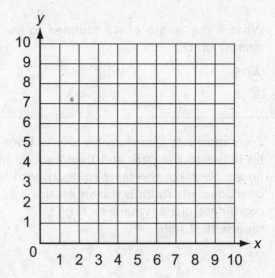

10 A right triangle is formed by the origin, the point $(0, 7)$, and a point in Quadrant I that is 25 units from the origin. What is the area of the triangle in square units?

_____

11 What is the distance to the nearest tenth of a unit between the points $(4, 1)$ and $(-8, 3)$?

_____

© Houghton Mifflin Harcourt Publishing Company

1 Ananya drew a cylinder with a radius of
3 inches and a height of 5 inches. She
also drew a cone with the same radius
and height. Which of the following is true?

Ⓐ The volume of the cone is four-thirds
the volume of the cylinder.

Ⓑ The volume of the cylinder is four-thirds
the volume of the cone.

Ⓒ The volume of the cone is three times
the volume of the cylinder.

Ⓓ The volume of the cylinder is three
times the volume of the cone.

2 A sphere has a radius of 3 centimeters.
What is the volume of the sphere in cubic
centimeters?

Ⓐ 27π

Ⓑ 36π

Ⓒ 216π

Ⓓ 288π

3 A sphere has a radius of 1 inch. What is the
volume of the sphere, in cubic inches?

Ⓐ $\frac{3}{4}$π   Ⓒ $\frac{4}{3}$π

Ⓑ π   Ⓓ 4π

4 The volume of a cone is 300 cubic
centimeters. A cylinder has the same radius
and height as the cone. What is the volume
of the cylinder?

Ⓐ 100 cm³   Ⓒ 900 cm³

Ⓑ 400 cm³   Ⓓ 1,200 cm³

5 A can of soup has the shape of a cylinder.
The diameter of the base of the can is
3.4 inches, and the height of the can is
4.5 inches. What is the volume of the can
rounded to the nearest tenth of a cubic
inch?

_____

6 Stefan is making a two-tier cake in
the shape shown. The diameter of the
bottom cylindrical tier is 8 inches, and
the diameter of the top cylindrical tier is
5 inches.

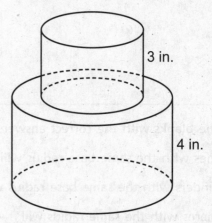

3 in.

4 in.

Which are the volumes of each tier and the
entire cake rounded to the nearest
cubic inch?

Select **all** the correct answers.

Ⓐ 59 in.³

Ⓑ 201 in.³

Ⓒ 236 in.³

Ⓓ 260 in.³

Ⓔ 804 in.³

Ⓕ 1,040 in.³

Name _____

7 A cylindrical can of cat food has a radius of 3.5 inches and a height of 1.25 inches. A second brand of cat food is packaged in a cylindrical can with a radius of 1.2 inches and a height of 1.25 inches. In terms of π, what is the difference in the volumes of the cans to the nearest ten-thousandth of a cubic inch?

The difference in the volumes of the cans

is _____ π in.^{3}

8 Consider a cone with the dimensions shown.

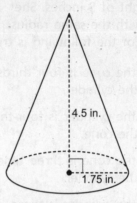

4.5 in.

1.75 in.

What is the volume of the cone rounded to the nearest tenth of a cubic inch?

(A) 8.2 in.^{3} (C) 43.3 in.^{3}

(B) 14.4 in.^{3} (D) 57.7 in.^{3}

9 Fill in the blanks with the correct answers from the list.

Two cones with the same base radius will _____ have the same volume.

Two cylinders with the same base radius will _____ have the same volume.

Two spheres with the same radius will _____ have the same volume.

| always | sometimes | never |

10 The base diameters of a cone and a cylinder, and the diameter of a sphere, are all 12 centimeters. The heights of the cone and cylinder are both 16 centimeters. What are the volumes of the cone, cylinder, and sphere rounded to the nearest hundredth of a cubic centimeter?

Place an X in the table to match each figure with its volume.

	603.19 cm^3	904.78 cm^3	1,809.56 cm^3	2,411.52 cm^3
Cone				
Cylinder				
Sphere				

1 Consider the scatter plot and trend line shown.

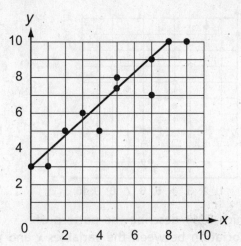

Which BEST describes the relationship between the two variables?

(A) no association

(B) quadratic association

(C) positive linear association

(D) negative linear association

2 Lisa analyzed the scatter plot shown.

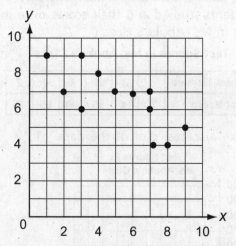

Which BEST describes the relationship between the two variables?

(A) no association

(B) nonlinear association

(C) positive linear association

(D) negative linear association

3 Consider the following scatter plot.

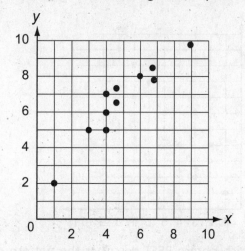

Which is not shown on the scatter plot?

(A) a cluster

(B) a linear association

(C) a positive association

(D) a negative association

4 A scatter plot is shown.

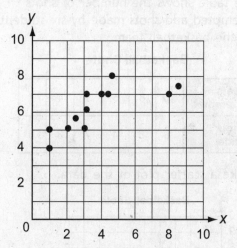

For the data shown in the scatter plot, which point is an outlier?

(A) (1, 4)

(B) (3, 3)

(C) (4, 7)

(D) (8, 7)

5 A scatter plot is shown.

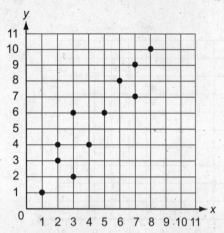

Which phrase BEST describes the pattern of association between the variables *x* and *y* shown in the scatter plot?

(A) no association

(B) a positive, linear association

(C) a negative, linear association

(D) a positive, nonlinear association

---

6 The table shows the number of shots attempted and shots made by six students on the basketball team.

Basketball Shots

Shots Attempted	10	8	5	9	4	7
Shots Made	1	6	4	7	3	5

Make a scatter plot of the data.

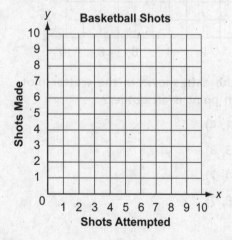

7 A scatter plot is shown.

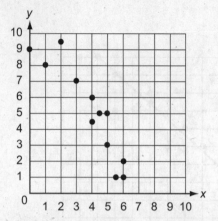

Which BEST describe the pattern of association between the variables *x* and *y* shown in the scatter plot?

Select **all** the correct answers.

(A) no association

(B) linear association

(C) positive association

(D) negative association

(E) nonlinear association

---

8 The table shows the number of hours students studied and their scores on a math test in Ms. Abuke's class.

Test Scores in Ms. Abuke's Class

Hours Studied	1	3	3	4	4	2
Test Score	70	80	85	90	85	75

Make a scatter plot of the data.

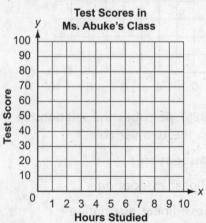

1 Which scatter plot has a trend line with a negative slope and all data points close to the trend line?

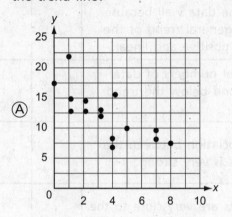

Ⓐ

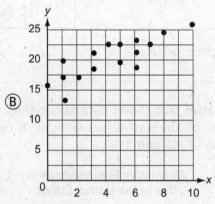

Ⓑ

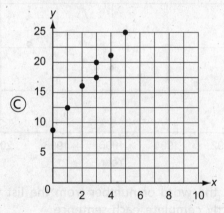

Ⓒ

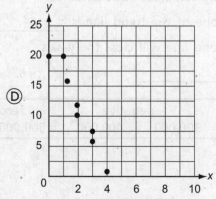

Ⓓ

2 The scatter plot shows the data for the number of hours Grace jogs each week for 8 weeks and the number of miles she jogs.

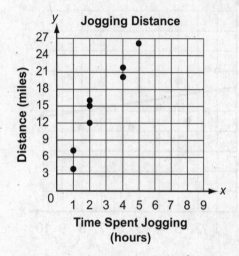

How can the slope of a trend line for the data be described?

Ⓐ negative slope that is greater than −1

Ⓑ negative slope that is less than −1

Ⓒ positive slope that is greater than 1

Ⓓ positive slope that is less than 1

3 A scatter plot is shown.

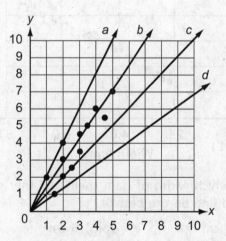

Which line best fits the data shown in the scatter plot?

Ⓐ line *a*

Ⓑ line *b*

Ⓒ line *c*

Ⓓ line *d*

Name _____

4 A scatter plot is shown.

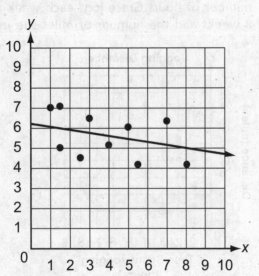

	True	False
The line fits the data well because it follows the general trend of the data, which is positive and linear.		
There are equal numbers of data points above and below the trend line.		
The linear association between the x- and y-values is very strong.		
The data points are very close to the trend line.		

Place an X in the table to show whether each statement is true or false.

---

5 The scatter plot shows lengths and widths of butter clam shells that were collected in Puget Sound.

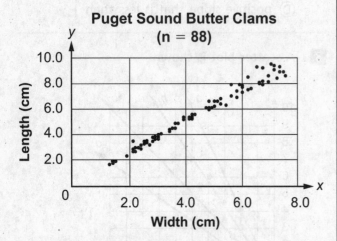

For which width of clam shells will the trend line be the best fit?

Ⓐ 0 cm   Ⓒ 6 cm

Ⓑ 3 cm   Ⓓ 7 cm

6 The scatter plot shows data about the number of alternative fuel vehicles in use between 1993 and 1999.

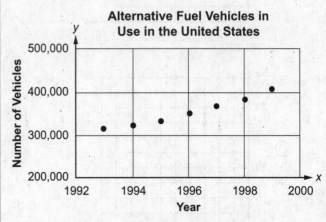

Select the word or number from the list to correctly complete each sentence.

The slope of the trend line is _____.

The trend line will cross the y-axis

near _____.

positive	negative		zero
200,000	300,000	400,000	500,000

1 Melvin analyzed prices of laptop computers based on the speed of the processor. He calculated the trend line to be represented by the equation shown, where x is the speed of the processor in gigahertz and y is the price in dollars.

$$y = 103x + 205$$

Which amount is closest to the price of a laptop with a processor speed of 2.0 gigahertz?

Ⓐ $308

Ⓑ $411

Ⓒ $513

Ⓓ $616

2 The scatter plot shows the distance traveled, d, in miles after filling a car's fuel tank and the amount of gasoline, g, in gallons left in the tank.

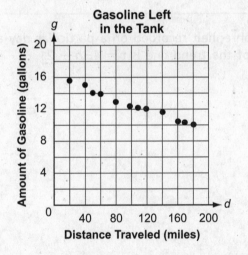

Gasoline Left in the Tank

The equation of a trend line for the data is $g = -\frac{1}{30}d + 16$. According to the trend line, how much gas is in the fuel tank when it is full?

Ⓐ 14 gal   Ⓒ 30 gal

Ⓑ 16 gal   Ⓓ 46 gal

3 Ms. Jackson asked each of her students how much time, t, in hours they studied for a test. She paired these numbers with the students' test scores, s, and created the scatter plot shown.

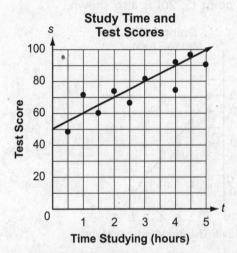

Study Time and Test Scores

The equation of the trend line is $s = 9t + 50$. In general, how does a student's score change for each additional hour of studying?

Ⓐ It increases by 9 points.

Ⓑ It decreases by 9 points.

Ⓒ It increases by 50 points.

Ⓓ It decreases by 50 points.

4 Colby graphed a scatter plot of student exam scores, y, and the number of hours each student had slept the night before the exam, x. She drew the trend line and calculated its equation to be $y = \frac{9}{2}x + 60$.

If a student slept 6 hours the night before the exam, what is the student's predicted score on the exam?

5 The scatter plot shows the relationship between the average number of times, t, a person goes to a movie theater per month and the person's age, a, in years for 9 people. A trend line that passes through the point (5, 20) is also shown.

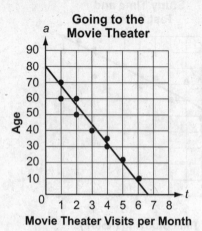

Going to the Movie Theater

What is the equation for the trend line?

_____

_____

6 The scatter plot shows the relationship between the number of pages, p, in each issue for 12 issues of a magazine and the number of full-page ads, a, in the magazine.

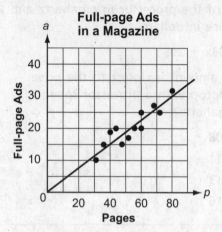

Full-page Ads in a Magazine

According to the trend line, what percentage of the pages are full-page ads?

Ⓐ 33.0%   Ⓒ 38.8%

Ⓑ 37.5%   Ⓓ 41.7%

---

7 The scatter plot shows the temperature, t, in degrees Fahrenheit recorded on a particular day at various times, h, in hours since 6:00 a.m. The equation of the trend line is $t = 4.3h + 21$.

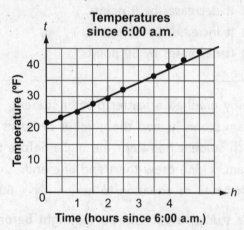

Temperatures since 6:00 a.m.

Place an X in the table to match each description with its value.

	8:30 a.m.	11:30 a.m.	21°F	33.9°F
The time to the nearest half hour at which the temperature reached freezing (32°F)				
The temperature at 6:00 a.m.				
The temperature at 9:00 a.m.				

1 Marlo collected data from students and adults about whether they watched the basketball game. The table shows the results of Marlo's survey.

	Watched	Did Not Watch	Total
Students	80	20	100
Adults	40	60	100
Total	120	80	200

Of the adults surveyed, how many watched the basketball game?

Ⓐ 40

Ⓑ 80

Ⓒ 100

Ⓓ 120

2 A chef collects data on customers' water orders and whether they order salad or soup. The results are shown in the table.

	Salad	Soup	Total
Plain Water	135	30	165
Water with Lemon	45	90	135
Total	180	120	300

Using the data in the table, which statement is true?

Ⓐ More customers order soup than salad.

Ⓑ More customers who drink water with lemon order salad instead of soup.

Ⓒ There is no association between customers' water orders and whether they order salad or soup.

Ⓓ There is an association between customers' water orders and whether they order salad or soup.

3 Students are asked if they prefer watching sunrise or sunset, and if they prefer camping or going to the beach. The data are shown in the table.

	Camping	Beach	Total
Sunrise	36	52	88
Sunset	24	38	62
Total	60	90	150

What percentage of students prefer watching sunrise given that they prefer going to the beach?

Ⓐ 41%   Ⓒ 58%

Ⓑ 42%   Ⓓ 59%

4 In a poll, 200 people were asked if they prefer rock or country music. The length of their shirt sleeves was also recorded. The data are shown in the table.

	Rock	Country	Total
Short Sleeves	75	50	125
Long Sleeves	45	30	75
Total	120	80	200

What is the joint relative frequency of people who prefer rock and wear long sleeves?

Ⓐ 0.225

Ⓑ 0.375

Ⓒ 0.45

Ⓓ 0.6

5 West Junior High track club has members
that run either the hurdles or in relay races.
No student runs in both. The data are
shown in the table.

	Hurdles	Relays	Total
Boys	8	12	20
Girls	15	15	30
Total	23	27	50

What is the joint relative frequency to the
nearest hundredth of boys who run relays?

_____

6 A store tested two marketing ideas by
offering a pair of items for sale for two
months. Each item was marked 50% off one
month and marked "Buy 1, Get 1 Free" the
other month. The number of items sold
each month is shown in the table.

	50% Off	Buy 1, Get 1 Free	Total
Item 1	12	8	20
Item 2	20	10	30
Total	32	18	50

What is the conditional relative frequency
to the nearest hundredth of selling item 2
given that the price was 50% off?

_____

7 There were 80 teenagers in line for tickets
to a concert. Tickets were $10 or $15.
Complete the frequency table for the tickets
the boys and girls purchased.

	$10	$15	Total
Boys		18	
Girls	26	22	
Total	40	40	80

8 Jordan asked 100 students at her school if
they prefer cats or dogs. She also recorded
their grade level. The data are shown in
the table.

	Prefer Cats	Prefer Dogs	Total
Seventh Grade	8	38	46
Eighth Grade	24	30	54
Total	32	68	100

Select **all** the correct statements.

(A) A surveyed student is more likely to
prefer dogs to cats.

(B) An eighth grade student is more likely
to prefer dogs to cats.

(C) Seventh grade students are less likely
than eighth grade students to prefer cats.

(D) Eighth grade students are more likely
than seventh grade students to prefer
dogs.

(E) Seventh grade students are equally as
likely as eighth grade students to prefer
dogs.

9 Tina collected data from students about
the type of book and fruit they preferred.
The two-way relative frequency table
shows the results of Tina's survey.

	Fiction	Nonfiction	Total
Apples	0.4	0.1	0.5
Grapes	0.3	0.2	0.5
Total	0.7	0.3	1.0

What is the marginal relative frequency of
students surveyed who prefer nonfiction?

(A) 0.1   (C) 0.3

(B) 0.2   (D) 0.5

Practice Test

Item	Content Focus	DOK	Record
1	Perform operations with numbers expressed in scientific notation.	2	
2	Describe a sequence of transformations relating two congruent figures.	2	
3	Know and apply the properties of integer exponents.	1	
4	Describe the effect of transformations using coordinates.	2	
5	Compare properties of functions each represented in a different way.	2	
6	Understand that rational and irrational numbers have decimal expansions.	1	
7	Use numbers expressed in scientific notation to estimate quantities.	1	
8	Use rational approximations of irrational numbers to compare their sizes.	2	
9	Model a linear relationship between two quantities.	3	
10	Construct and interpret scatter plots.	2	
11	Analyze and solve pairs of simultaneous linear equations.	2	
12	Understand that a function assigns to each input exactly one output.	2	
13	Describe a sequence of transformations relating two similar figures.	2	
14	Derive the equations $y = mx$ and $y = mx + b$.	2	
15	Use a linear model to solve problems for bivariate measurement data.	2	
16	Apply the Pythagorean Theorem to determine unknown side lengths.	2	
17	Interpret the equation $y = mx + b$ as defining a linear function.	2	
18	Know the formulas for the volumes of cones, cylinders, and spheres.	2	
19	Solve linear equations in one variable.	2	
20	Explain a proof of the Pythagorean Theorem and its converse.	2	
21	Construct and interpret frequency and relative frequency tables.	3	
22	Describe the relationship between two quantities by analyzing a graph. Sketch a graph of a function that has been described verbally.	2	
23	Know facts about angles of triangles, facts about angles created when parallel lines are cut by a transversal, and the AA similarity criterion.	2	
24	Compare proportional relationships represented in different ways.	2	
25	Apply the Pythagorean Theorem to find the distance between two points.	1	
26	Fit a line to a scatter plot and informally assess the fit.	2	
27	Solve equations of the form $x^2 = p$ and $x^3 = p$.	1	
28	Interpret the equation $y = mx + b$ as defining a linear function.	2	

Item	Content Focus	DOK	Record
29	Verify experimentally the properties of rotations, reflections, and translations.	2	
30	Analyze and solve pairs of simultaneous linear equations.	2	
31	Model a linear relationship between two quantities.	3	
32	Compare properties of functions each represented in a different way.	2	
33	Solve linear equations in one variable.	2	
34	Solve problems leading to two linear equations in two variables.	3	
35	Solve problems involving volumes of cones.	3	
36	Compare proportional relationships represented in different ways.	3	
37	Solve problems related to angle pairs.	3	
38	Interpret the equation $y = mx + b$ as defining a linear function.	3	
39	Describe a sequence of transformations relating two similar figures.	3	

1 An expression is shown.

$$\frac{(7 \times 10^{-6}) + (8 \times 10^{-6})}{5 \times 10^{8}}$$

Which expression is equivalent?

Ⓐ 3×10^{-20} Ⓒ 3×10^{-2}

Ⓑ 3×10^{-14} Ⓓ 3×10^{14}

2 Select **all** the sequences of transformations that produce a figure that is congruent to the original figure.

Ⓐ a translation and then a reflection

Ⓑ a reflection and then a dilation

Ⓒ a dilation and then a rotation

Ⓓ a rotation and then a reflection

Ⓔ a translation and then a dilation

Ⓕ a rotation and then a translation

3 What is the value of $2^2 \cdot 2^{-4}$?

Ⓐ 64

Ⓑ 4

Ⓒ $\frac{1}{4}$

Ⓓ $\frac{1}{256}$

4 The quadrilateral shown is reflected in the y-axis and then translated 3 units up.

Draw the quadrilateral after its transformations.

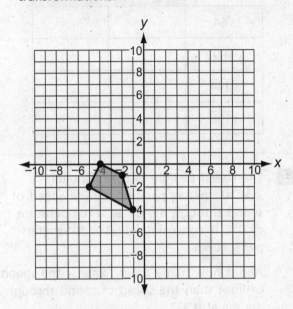

5 A function is represented by the table.

x	y
−3	−11
0	−2
3	7

Which function has a rate of change that is equal to the rate of change of the function represented by the table?

Ⓐ $y = \frac{1}{4}x - 11$

Ⓑ $y = 2x + 1$

Ⓒ $y = 3x + 8$

Ⓓ $y = \frac{7}{2}x + 3$

6 Place an X in the table to show whether each number is rational or irrational.

	Rational	Irrational
$\sqrt{64}$		
$\sqrt{80}$		
$\sqrt{144}$		
$\sqrt{150}$		

7 The speed of light is approximately 3×10^8 meters per second. The speed of sound through dry air at a temperature of 0°C is approximately 3×10^2 meters per second.

About how many times faster is the speed of light than the speed of sound through dry air at 0°C?

Ⓐ 30,000,000,000

Ⓑ 10,000,000,000

Ⓒ 3,000,000

Ⓓ 1,000,000

8 Plot the numbers $\sqrt{3}$, $\sqrt{6}$, and $\sqrt{12}$ at their approximate locations on the number line.

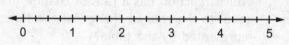

9 Jovian's daily salary, S, based on the number of hours he works, h, is shown in the table.

Hours Worked (h)	Daily Salary (S)
3	$135
5	$185
6	$210
9	$285

Part A

Which equation represents this function?

Ⓐ $S = 25h + 60$

Ⓑ $S = 45h$

Ⓒ $S = 50h - 15$

Ⓓ $S = 75h - 90$

Part B

Rey's daily salary is modeled by the function $S = 35h + 15$.

Fill in the blanks with the correct words from the lists.

Rey earns _____ than Jovian for 8 hours of work.

more   less

I know this because the _____ of Rey's function is _____ than the _____ of Jovian's function when $t = 8$.

slope   y-intercept   value
greater   less

10 A scatter plot is shown.

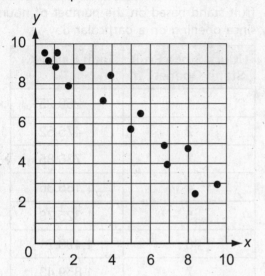

Which statement is true for the given scatter plot?

(A) The data show a nonlinear association.

(B) The data show no association.

(C) The data show a positive correlation.

(D) The data show a negative correlation.

11 A system of linear equations is shown.

$$2x + 4y = 16$$

$$2x = 5y - 11$$

What is the solution to the given system of linear equations?

(A) $(-2, 5)$ (C) $(7, 5)$

(B) $(2, 3)$ (D) $(10, -1)$

12 The graph of a function is shown.

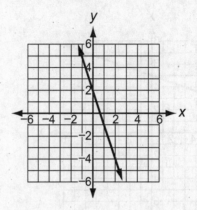

Fill in the table to show the relationship between x and y in the function.

x	y
1	
0	
	−4

13 Which sequence of transformations results in figures that are similar but not congruent?

(A) dilation with a factor of 2, translation 6 units down

(B) translation 4 units up, 120° counterclockwise rotation

(C) reflection in the y-axis, translation 7 units to the right

(D) 45° clockwise rotation, reflection in the x-axis

14 The graph of a linear function is shown.

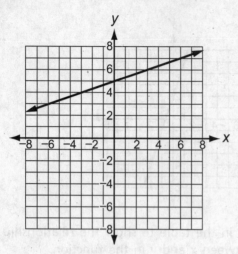

Fill in the blanks with the correct numbers from the list.

For the function shown, the y-intercept is

_____ , and the slope is _____ .

| 5 | 3 | $\frac{2}{3}$ | $\frac{1}{3}$ | $\frac{1}{4}$ |

15 The table shows the total sales at a local fruit stand based on the number of hours since opening on a particular day.

Hours Since Fruit Stand Opened, h	Total Sales ($), T
1	250.25
2	475.52
3	736.85
4	1,185.36
5	1,325.78
6	1,400.71
7	1,859.43
8	2,027.95

The line of best fit for the data is
$T = 255.90h + 6.19$.

What is the meaning of the slope in terms of the context?

Ⓐ The fruit stand makes approximately $6.19 per hour.

Ⓑ The fruit stand started the day with approximately $6.19.

Ⓒ The fruit stand makes approximately $255.90 per hour.

Ⓓ The fruit stand started the day with approximately $255.90.

16 Fill in the blank with a number from the list to correctly complete the sentence.

Triangle *ABC* is a right triangle. The length of the hypotenuse is 50 inches, and the length of one leg is 40 inches. The length of the other leg is _____ inches.

10	30	64	900

17 At the local bowling alley, it costs $6 per day to rent shoes and $3 per game to bowl.

What is true about the function that represents the total cost to bowl, including a shoe rental?

Ⓐ It is nonlinear because the graph of the function does not go through the origin.

Ⓑ It is nonlinear because the graph of the function is not a straight line.

Ⓒ It is linear because the graph of the function goes through the origin.

Ⓓ It is linear because the graph of the function is a straight line.

18 The base of a cone has a diameter of 8 centimeters. The height of the cone is 9 centimeters.

What is the approximate volume of the cone? Use 3.14 for π.

Ⓐ 1,808.64 cubic centimeters

Ⓑ 602.88 cubic centimeters

Ⓒ 452.16 cubic centimeters

Ⓓ 150.72 cubic centimeters

19 Place an X in the table to show the number of solutions for each equation.

	No Solutions	One Solution	Infinitely Many Solutions
$4 + 5x = 5x + 4$			
$5x + 4 = -2 + 5x$			
$5x + 4 = 4x + 5$			

20 Select **all** the sets of side lengths that can form a right triangle.

Ⓐ 5 cm, 7 cm, 10 cm

Ⓑ 5 in., 12 in., 13 in.

Ⓒ 7 ft, 9 ft, 11 ft

Ⓓ 8 m, 15 m, 17 m

Ⓔ 9 mm, 12 mm, 15 mm

21 In a survey, 400 students were asked whether they prefer fruit or vegetables. The partially completed table shown displays the results.

	Fruit	Vegetables	Total
Boys		98	
Girls			230
Total	244	156	

How many more girls prefer fruit than boys?

Ⓐ 100   Ⓒ 60

Ⓑ 88   Ⓓ 40

22 The graph represents the 30-minute run Johnny took today. The x-axis shows the time from the start of the run. The y-axis shows the total distance traveled.

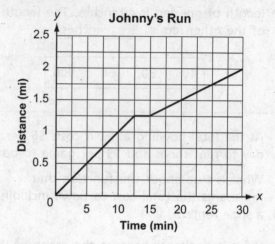

Johnny's Run

Part A

After how many minutes did Johnny stop running for the first time?

Johnny stopped running after _____ minutes.

Part B

Circle the correct answer to complete the sentence.

In the first part of the run, Johnny ran faster / slower than in the last part of the run.

23 What is the measure of ∠x, in degrees, in the figure shown?

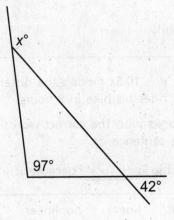

m∠x = _____ °

24 The graph of a proportional relationship and an equation are shown.

Graph:

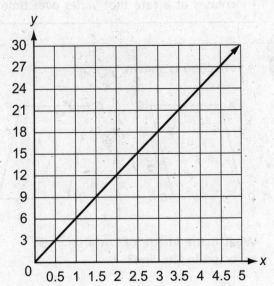

Equation: $y = \frac{10}{3}x + 8$

What is the greater unit rate?

Ⓐ 3   Ⓒ 6

Ⓑ $\frac{10}{3}$ Ⓓ 8

25 A graph of two points is shown.

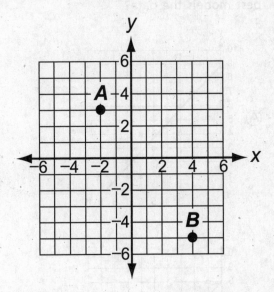

What is the distance between point A and point B?

Ⓐ 6 units

Ⓑ 8 units

Ⓒ 10 units

Ⓓ 14 units

26 Which scatter plot shows a line of fit that best models the data?

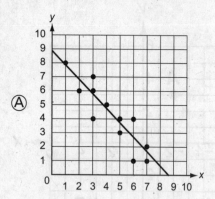

Ⓐ

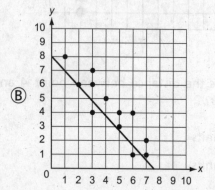

Ⓑ

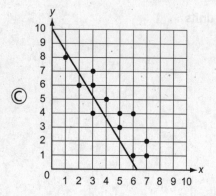

Ⓒ

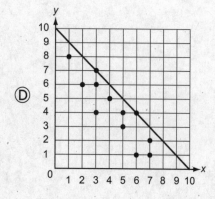

Ⓓ

27 A cube with an edge of length s has a volume of 125 cubic units. What is the value of s?

$s =$ _____ units

28 The function $y = 10.5x$ models the distance in miles Raja rides his bike in x hours.

Fill in the blanks with the correct words to complete the sentence.

This relationship is _____ because it

| constant | linear | nonlinear |

_____ .

is always increasing

increases at a constant rate

increases at a rate that varies over time

29 A reflection is shown.

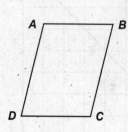 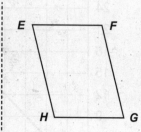

What is the image of $\overline{DA}$ after it is reflected in the line?

Ⓐ $\overline{EF}$

Ⓑ $\overline{GF}$

Ⓒ $\overline{HG}$

Ⓓ $\overline{HE}$

30 Analyze the system of equations shown.

$y = 5(2x + 1)$

$y = 2(5x + 1)$

Circle the number of solutions that this system of equations has.

• No solution
• One solution
• Infinitely many solutions

31 The table shows the total amount, T, in Henry's savings account after m months.

Months Since Opening, m	Total Amount ($), T
2	260
4	360
5	410
7	510

Fill in the blanks with the correct answers to complete the sentences.

The _____ is the amount of money that was used to open the account, which is _____.

The _____ is the amount of money that was added to the account each month, which is _____.

initial value	rate of change
$50 $60	$160 $260

32 The equation and the table show two linear functions.

Function A:

x	y
−6	3
0	4
12	6

Function B: $y = \frac{5}{2}x + 9$

What is the rate of change of the function that has the greater rate of change?

Ⓐ $\frac{1}{6}$

Ⓑ $\frac{5}{2}$

Ⓒ 6

Ⓓ 9

33 Which equation has infinitely many solutions?

Ⓐ $4x - 10 = -2(-2x + 5)$

Ⓑ $2(3x - 10) = 6x + 20$

Ⓒ $-7x + 9 = 9x - 7$

Ⓓ $-16 + 3x = 3x + 16$

34 An animal rescue organization transported 354 dogs and cats to a new facility in trailers and vans. Each trailer transported a total of 55 animals. Each van transported a total of 12 animals. There were 4 more trailers than vans.

- What is the total number of animals that were transported in trailers?
- What is the total number of animals that were transported in vans?
- Explain your reasoning and show your work.

Enter your answer and explanation in the space provided. Support your answer using words, numbers, and/or symbols.

35 The circular base of a cone has a center C. Another circle, with center B, is parallel to the base. This circle is the base of a smaller cone with height AB. Triangle ABD is similar to triangle ACE. The smaller cone is removed from Figure 1 to create Figure 2, as shown. The measurements in the diagram are given in centimeters.

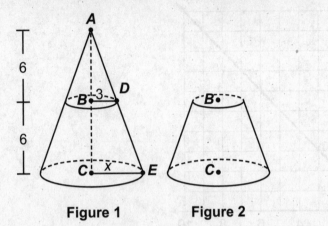

Figure 1   **Figure 2**

• What is the value of x, the radius of the larger cone?

• What is the volume of Figure 2? Round your answer to the nearest tenth.

• Explain your reasoning and show your work.

Enter your answer in the space provided. Explain your answer using words, numbers, and/or symbols.

36 The table and the graph below show Beth's and Scott's wages, respectively, based on the number of hours worked.

Beth's Wages

Hours Worked	Wages ($)
5	83.75
7	117.25
9	150.75

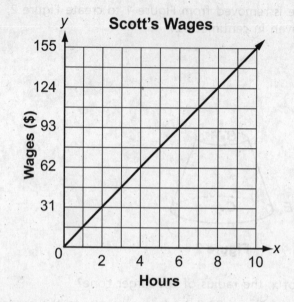

Last year, Beth and Scott each worked 8 hours per day and 5 days each week.

Beth claims that after working 10 weeks, she earned $500 more than Scott.

Is Beth correct? Explain why or why not.

Enter your answer in the space provided. Explain your answer using words, numbers, and/or symbols.

37 In the figure below, line ℓ is parallel to line m. The lines are intersected by a transversal.

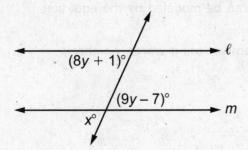

Write a system of linear equations that can be used to determine the values of x and y, and explain why your system is correct.

Then solve for x and y, and explain how you solved the problem.

Enter your answer and explanation in the space provided. Support your answer using words, numbers, and/or symbols.

38 Write one linear equation and one nonlinear equation. Explain why each equation is linear or nonlinear. Then, describe a real-world situation that can be modeled by the equation $y = 15x + 9$.

Enter your answer in the space provided. Explain your answer using words, numbers, and/or symbols.

39 Rectangle *EFGH* is shown on the coordinate plane.

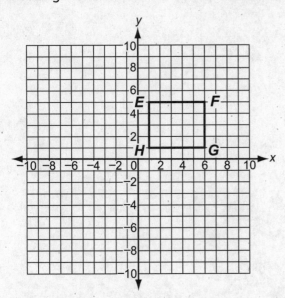

Rectangle *EFGH* undergoes a dilation, then a translation, resulting in Rectangle *E′F′G′H′* (not shown). The length of side *E′H′* is 8 units. The coordinates of vertex *E′* are (6, 10) and the coordinates of vertex *G′* are (16, 2).

• Describe the dilation and the translation.

• Explain your reasoning.

Enter your answer and explanation in the space provided. Justify your answer using words, numbers, and/or symbols.

This page intentionally
left blank.

1 An expression is shown.

$$\frac{(9 \times 10^{-9}) + (5 \times 10^{-9})}{2 \times 10^6}$$

Which expression is equivalent?

Ⓐ 7×10^{15}

Ⓑ 7×10^{-3}

Ⓒ 7×10^{-15}

Ⓓ 7×10^{-24}

---

2 Triangles *ABC* and *DEF* are shown.

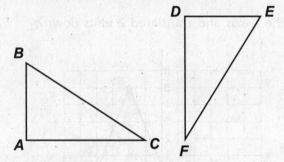

Which transformations of triangle *ABC* produce triangle *DEF*?

Ⓐ a reflection and then a rotation

Ⓑ a translation and then a reflection

Ⓒ a rotation and then a translation

Ⓓ a horizontal translation and then a vertical translation

---

3 Which expressions are equivalent to $\frac{1}{9}$?

Select all the correct expressions.

Ⓐ $3^3 \times 3^{-5}$

Ⓑ -3^2

Ⓒ $3^2 \times 3^{-4}$

Ⓓ 9^{-1}

Ⓔ -9^1

4 Triangle *ABC* is shown.

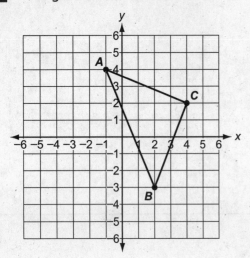

Which graph shows triangle *ABC* reflected across the *x*-axis and translated 2 units down?

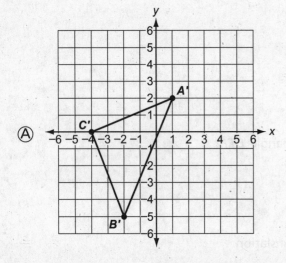

Ⓐ

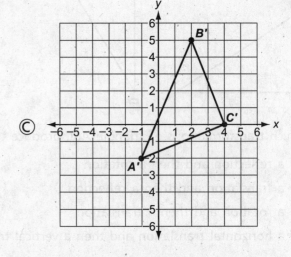

Ⓒ

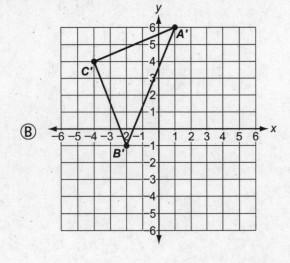

Ⓑ

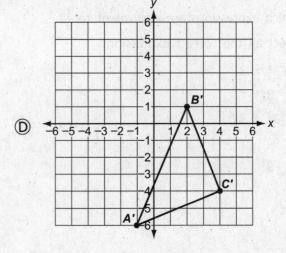

Ⓓ

5 Two functions are shown.

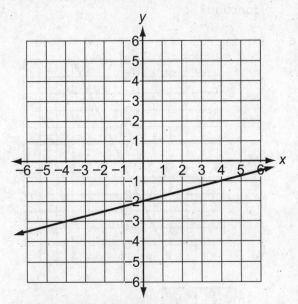

x	y
−4	−5
0	3
4	11

What is the greater rate of change of these two functions?

_____

6 Which number is a rational number?

Ⓐ $\sqrt{63}$ Ⓒ $\sqrt{121}$

Ⓑ $\sqrt{72}$ Ⓓ $\sqrt{250}$

7 The mass of Mercury is approximately 3×10^{23} kilograms. The mass of Saturn is approximately 6×10^{26} kilograms. About how many times more mass does Saturn have than Mercury?

_____

8 What is the approximate value of $\sqrt{7}$?

Ⓐ 2.56   Ⓒ 3.05

Ⓑ 2.65   Ⓓ 3.50

9 Edward is having a birthday party at a bowling alley. The total cost to have the party, y, based on the number of people attending the party, x, is shown in the table.

Number of People (x)	Total Cost (y)
5	$85
7	$95
10	$110
20	$160

Part A

Write an equation to represent the total cost to have the party, y, in terms of the number of people attending the party, x.

_____

Part B

Fill in the blanks with answers from the list to correctly complete the sentences.

The cost per person is represented by the _____ of the function and is _____ per person.

The upfront cost for booking a party, no matter how many people are attending, is represented by the _____ of the function and is _____.

initial value		rate of change			
$2	$5	$10	$35	$60	$85

10 A scatter plot is shown.

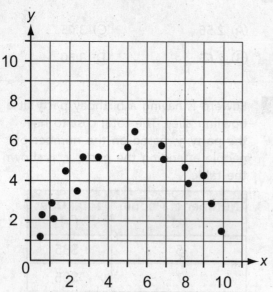

Which statement is true for the given scatter plot?

Ⓐ The data show a nonlinear association.

Ⓑ The data show no association.

Ⓒ The data show only a positive correlation.

Ⓓ The data show only a negative correlation.

11 Place an X in the table to show whether each system of equations has no solution, one solution, or infinitely many solutions.

	No Solution	One Solution	Infinitely Many Solutions
$2x + 4y = 6$ $4x + 2y = 6$			
$y = x + 3$ $x = y - 3$			
$y = 3(2x - 4)$ $y = 2(3x - 4)$			

12 Which of these does not represent a function?

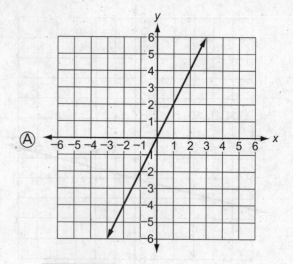

Ⓐ

x	y
−4	5
−2	6
0	7
1	5

Ⓑ

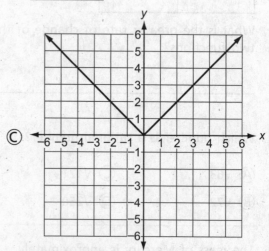

Ⓒ

x	y
−3	4
−1	7
−1	−2
4	0

Ⓓ

© Houghton Mifflin Harcourt Publishing Company

13 Triangle *ABC* is transformed to produce triangle *DEF* as shown.

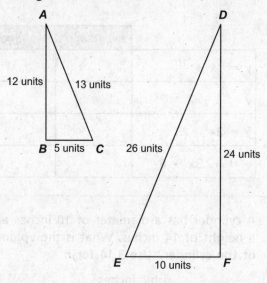

Select the **two** transformations that are involved.

Ⓐ rotation

Ⓑ reflection

Ⓒ vertical translation

Ⓓ dilation with a scale factor of 2

Ⓔ dilation with a scale factor of $\frac{1}{2}$

14 Which pair of triangles can be used to show that the slope of a line is the same anywhere along the line?

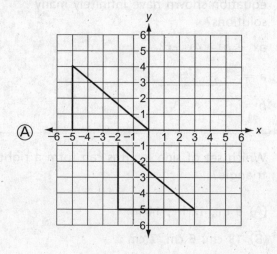

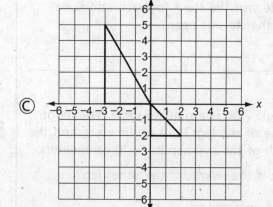

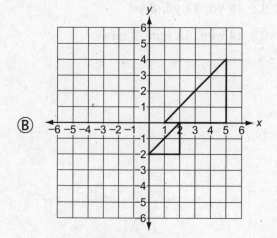

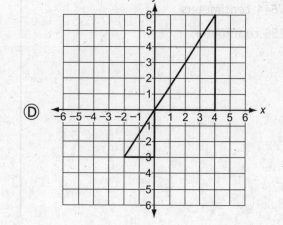

15 A store kept a running total of the number of people that visited it one day based on the number of hours it had been open. The table shows the data the store collected.

Hours Since Opening (x)	Number of People (y)
2	152
4	267
6	405
8	609
10	684
12	791

The approximate line of best fit for the data is $y = 66x + 20$. According to the line's equation, about how many more people visit the store for each additional hour the store is open?

_____

16 Triangle ABC is a right triangle. The length of one of the legs is 12 centimeters, and the length of the hypotenuse is 20 centimeters.

What is the length of the other leg?

- (A) $\sqrt{8}$ centimeters
- (B) 16 centimeters
- (C) $\sqrt{544}$ centimeters
- (D) 256 centimeters

17 Place an X in the table to show whether each function is linear or nonlinear.

	Linear	Nonlinear
$y = \frac{5}{2}x + \frac{10}{3}$		
$y = \frac{1}{x} + 2$		
$y = 2x^2 - 3$		
$y = -2.3x + 8$		

18 A cylinder has a diameter of 10 inches and a height of 14 inches. What is the volume of the cylinder? Use 3.14 for π.

_____ cubic inches

19 What values of a and b would make the equation shown have infinitely many solutions?

$ax + b = 4x + 3$

$a =$ _____

$b =$ _____

20 Which set of side lengths can form a right triangle?

- (A) 9 in., 12 in., 14 in.
- (B) 13 cm, 6 cm, 7 cm
- (C) 15 yd, 17 yd, 8 yd
- (D) 14 mm, 12 mm, 5 mm

21 In a survey, 500 students were asked whether they prefer milk or orange juice with breakfast. The table shown partially displays the results.

	Milk	Orange Juice	Total
Boys		139	
Girls			227
Total	206	294	

How many more boys than girls prefer milk?

---

22 Which graph represents a linear function decreasing at a constant rate?

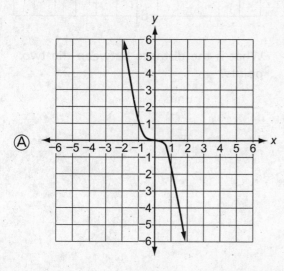

Ⓐ

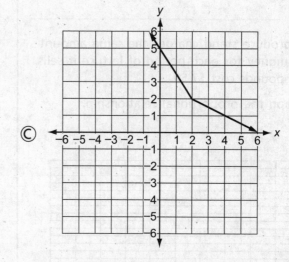

Ⓒ

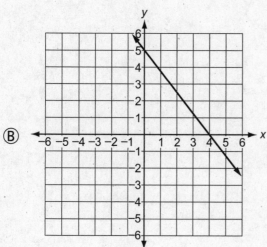

Ⓑ

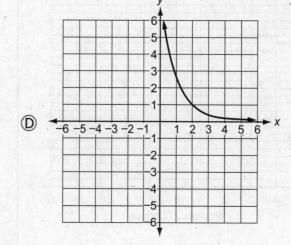

Ⓓ

23 In the figure shown, the line segments form a triangle.

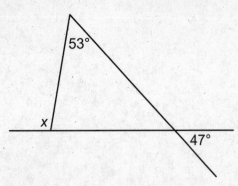

What is the measure of ∠x in the figure?

Ⓐ 47°

Ⓒ 100°

Ⓑ 80°

Ⓓ 133°

24 A produce stand charges the same amount of money for each pound of lettuce it sells. Six pounds cost $7.50.

Graph the proportional relationship.

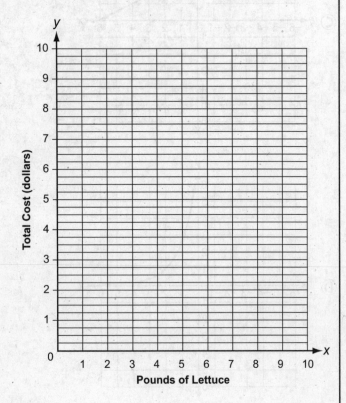

25 A graph of point A and point B is shown.

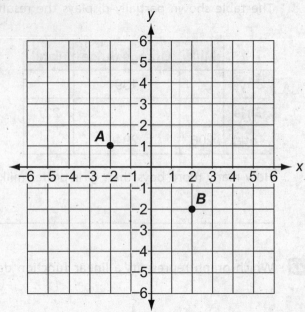

What is the distance between the two points?

_____ units

26 Which scatter plot shows a line that best models the data?

Ⓐ
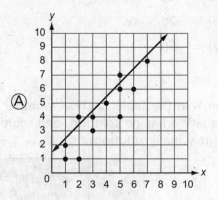

Ⓑ
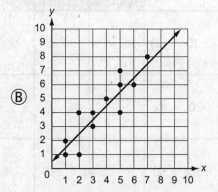

Ⓒ
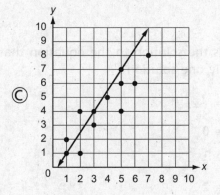

Ⓓ
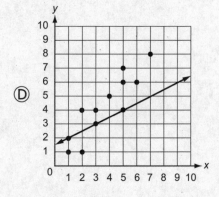

27 A square has an area of 0.81 square units. What is the side length of the square?

Ⓐ 0.09 units

Ⓑ 0.2025 units

Ⓒ 0.405 units

Ⓓ 0.9 units

28 Which **three** functions are nonlinear?

Ⓐ $y = 8 + 5.2x$

Ⓑ $y = 3^x + 9$

Ⓒ $y = 4.1x^2 + 17$

Ⓓ $y = -2.5x$

Ⓔ $y = (x - 5)^2$

29 Parallelogram *ABCD* is reflected across a vertical line to produce parallelogram *EFGH* as shown.

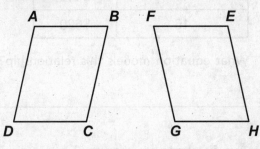

Which of the following statements is **true**?

Ⓐ $AD = EH$

Ⓑ $m\angle C = m\angle H$

Ⓒ $\overline{FG}$ is the image of $\overline{AD}$.

Ⓓ $\angle E$ is the image of $\angle B$.

30 Consider the following system of equations.

$3x = 2y - 7$

$3x + 4y = 5$

What is the solution to the system?

Ⓐ $(-1, 2)$ Ⓒ $(2, -1)$

Ⓑ $(1, 5)$ Ⓓ $(5, 1)$

---

31 The total cost, y, in dollars to repair a clock based on the number of hours it takes to fix it, x, is shown in the table.

Number of Hours (x)	Total Cost (y)
2	$130
5	$235
7	$305
11	$445
16	$620

What equation models this relationship?

---

32 Two functions are shown.

Function 1: $y = \frac{3}{2}x + 8$

Function 2:

x	y
−6	−1
0	1
12	5

What is the rate of change, in simplest form, of the function that has the lesser rate of change?

---

33 Three equations are given.

$-3x - 6 = -3(x - 2)$

$4(x - 5) = -20 + 4x$

$3(x - 2) = -3(x - 2)$

Part A

Place an X in the table to show whether each equation has no solution, one solution, or infinitely many solutions.

	No Solution	One Solution	Infinitely Many Solutions
$-3x - 6 = -3(x - 2)$			
$4(x - 5) = -20 + 4x$			
$3(x - 2) = -3(x - 2)$			

Part B

What is the solution to the equation that has only one solution?

Ⓐ $x = -2$

Ⓑ $x = 0$

Ⓒ $x = \frac{1}{2}$

Ⓓ $x = 2$

34 A baker sells a total of 592 cookies in one week. Cookies are sold in boxes and tins. Each tin of cookies contains 8 cookies Each box of cookies contains 24 cookies. The baker sold 6 more tins than boxes.

- What is the total number of cookies sold in boxes?
- What is the total number of cookies sold in tins?
- Explain your reasoning and show your work.

Enter your answer and explanation in the space provided. Support your answer using words, numbers, and/or symbols.

© Houghton Mifflin Harcourt Publishing Company

35 The circular base of a cone has a center C. Another circle, with center B, is parallel to the base. This circle is the base of a smaller cone with height AB. Triangle ABD is similar to triangle ACE. The smaller cone is removed from Figure 1 to create Figure 2, as shown. The measurements in the diagram are given in centimeters.

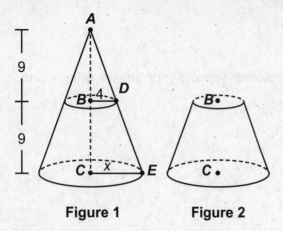

Figure 1   **Figure 2**

• What is the value of x, the radius of the larger cone?

• What is the volume of Figure 2? Round your answer to the nearest tenth.

• Explain your reasoning and show your work.

Enter your answer and explanation in the space provided. Justify your answer using words, numbers, and/or symbols.

36 The table and the graph below show Katy's and Bill's pay, respectively, based on the number of hours worked.

Katy's Wages

Hours Worked	Wages ($)
3	51.75
5	86.25
7	120.75

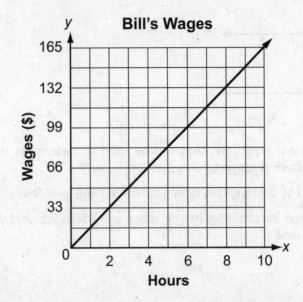

Bill's Wages

Last year, Katy and Bill each worked 10 hours per day and 5 days each week.

Katy claims that after 27 weeks she earned $1,000 more than Bill. Is Katy correct? Explain why or why not.

Enter your answer in the space provided. Explain your answer using words, numbers, and/or symbols.

37 In the figure below, line *m* is parallel to line *n*. The lines are intersected by a transversal.

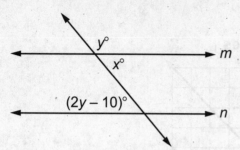

Write a system of linear equations that can be used to determine the values of *x* and *y*, and explain why your system is correct.

Then solve for *x* and *y*, and explain how you solved the problem.

Enter your answer and explanation in the space provided. Support your answer using words, numbers, and/or symbols.

38 Write one linear equation and one nonlinear equation. Explain why each equation is linear or nonlinear. Then, describe a real-world situation that can be modeled by the equation $y = 5x + 25$.

Enter your answer in the space provided. Explain your answer using words, numbers, and/or symbols.

39 Rectangle *WXYZ* is shown on the coordinate plane.

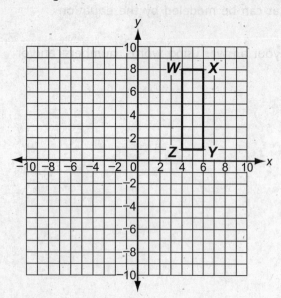

Rectangle *WXYZ* undergoes a dilation, then a reflection, resulting in Rectangle *W'X'Y'Z'* (not shown). The length of *W'X'* is 1 unit. The coordinates of vertex *W'* are (2, −4). The coordinates of vertex *Y'* are $\left(3, -\frac{1}{2}\right)$.

- Describe the dilation and the reflection.
- Explain your reasoning.

Enter your answer and explanation in the space provided. Justify your answer using words, numbers, and/or symbols.

1 An expression is shown.

$$\frac{(11 \times 10^{-7}) + (4 \times 10^{-7})}{3 \times 10^{3}}$$

Which expression is equivalent?

(A) 5×10^{-17} (C) 5×10^{-10}

(B) 5×10^{-11} (D) 5×10^{-4}

2 Triangles *ABC* and *DEF* are shown.

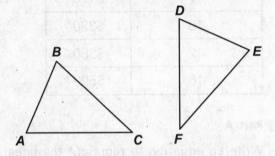

Which transformations of triangle *ABC* produce triangle *DEF*?

(A) a rotation and then a reflection

(B) a rotation and then a translation

(C) a translation and then a reflection

(D) a horizontal translation and then a vertical translation

3 An expression is shown.

$$3^{-3} \times 3^{2}$$

What is the value of the expression?

(A) $\frac{1}{729}$ (C) 3

(B) $\frac{1}{3}$ (D) 243

4 The quadrilateral on the coordinate plane below is reflected over the *x*-axis and then translated 4 units to the right.

Draw the quadrilateral after the transformations.

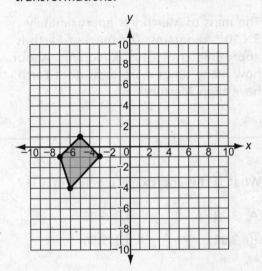

5 A function is represented by the graph.

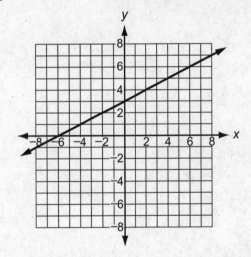

Which equation has a lesser rate of change than the graphed function?

(A) $y = \frac{3}{2}x - \frac{1}{4}$ (C) $y = \frac{1}{2}x + \frac{1}{10}$

(B) $y = \frac{1}{4}x + 12$ (D) $y = x - 5$

6 Which number is a rational number?

Ⓐ $\sqrt{46}$ Ⓒ $\sqrt{125}$

Ⓑ $\sqrt{80}$ Ⓓ $\sqrt{144}$

7 The mass of Mercury is approximately 3×10^{23} kilograms. The mass of Earth is approximately 6×10^{24} kilograms. About how many times more mass does Earth have than Mercury?

_____

8 What is the approximate value of $\sqrt{11}$?

Ⓐ 3.23   Ⓒ 5.05

Ⓑ 3.32   Ⓓ 5.50

9 Lori has a tutoring company that uses a linear model to determine the total cost in dollars to her customers based on the number of hours they want tutoring for the school year.

The table below shows the total cost of tutoring based on the number of hours.

Number of Hours (x)	Total Cost (y)
5	$170
10	$320
12	$380
16	$500

Part A

Write an equation to represent the linear model Lori uses to determine the total cost, y, for the school year to one of her customers based on the number of hours, x.

_____

Part B

Fill in the blanks with the correct answers from the list to complete the sentences.

The _____ is used to represent the amount Lori charges for 0 hours of tutoring. The value is _____ .

The _____ is used to represent the amount Lori charges per hour of tutoring. The value is _____ .

initial value		rate of change	
$5	$20	$30	$170

10 A scatter plot is shown for sales of hand warmers based on the temperature.

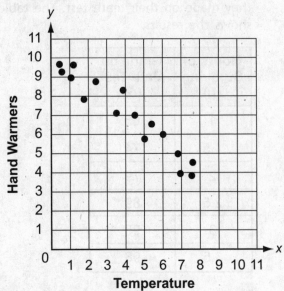

Select the **three** statements that correctly interpret the graph.

Ⓐ The data show a linear association.

Ⓑ The data show a nonlinear association.

Ⓒ The data show a positive correlation.

Ⓓ The data show a negative correlation.

Ⓔ There are no outliers for the data.

Ⓕ There are multiple outliers for the data.

11 A system of linear equations is shown.

$3x + 5y = -12$

$3x = 4y + 15$

What is the solution to the given system?

Ⓐ $(-9, 3)$ Ⓒ $(1, -3)$

Ⓑ $(-3, 1)$ Ⓓ $(5, 0)$

12 A graph of a function is shown.

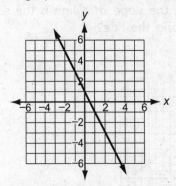

Fill in the table to show the relationship between *x* and *y* in the function.

x	y
–2	
0	
	–5

13 Triangle *ABC* is transformed to produce triangle *DEF* as shown.

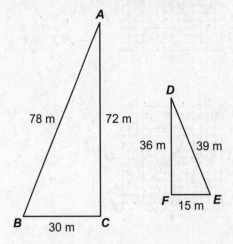

Select the **two** transformations that are involved.

Ⓐ rotation

Ⓑ reflection

Ⓒ vertical translation

Ⓓ dilation with a scale factor of 2

Ⓔ dilation with a scale factor of $\frac{1}{2}$

14 Which **three** pairs of triangles can be used to show that the slope of a line is the same anywhere along the line?

Ⓐ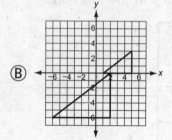

Ⓑ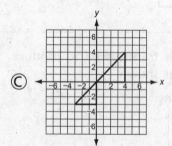

Ⓒ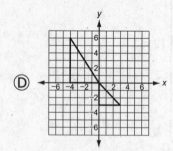

Ⓓ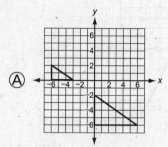

Ⓔ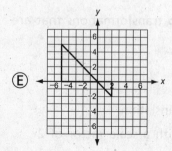

15 Six students who studied for different amounts of time were asked what grade they made on their math test. The table shows the results.

Hours of Studying (h)	Grade on Math Test (G)
1	65
1.5	74
2	79
2.5	89
3	95
3.5	98

The approximate line of best fit for the data is $G = 14h + 53$.

Which **three** statements correctly interpret the parts of the equation for the line of best fit?

Ⓐ The slope is 14.

Ⓑ The slope is 53.

Ⓒ The y-intercept is 14.

Ⓓ The y-intercept is 53.

Ⓔ The initial value shows that someone who did not study at all would likely get a 53 on the test.

Ⓕ The rate of change shows that someone who did not study at all would likely get a 53 on the test.

16 Triangle *ABC* is a right triangle. The length of one of the legs is 15 inches, and the length of the hypotenuse is 17 inches. What is the length in inches of the other leg?

17 Marcus opens his savings account with $100. He puts in $25 the first month after opening it. The following month, he puts in 3 times that amount. For each of the following 3 months, Marcus continues to triple the amount he puts into the account.

What is true about the function that represents the amount of money Marcus puts into the account based on the number of months it has been since he opened the account?

Ⓐ It is linear because the graph of the function is a straight line.

Ⓑ It is linear because the graph of the function goes through the origin.

Ⓒ It is nonlinear because the graph of the function is not a straight line.

Ⓓ It is nonlinear because the graph of the function does not go through the origin.

18 A cone has a base with a diameter of 12 inches and a height of 15 inches. What is the volume of the cone in cubic inches using 3.14 for π?

_____

19 Solve the equation shown for x.

$-3(x + 1) + 4(x + 1) = 3x + 9$

$x =$ _____

20 Which set of side lengths can form a right triangle?

Ⓐ 4 yd, 19 yd, 15 yd

Ⓑ 25 cm, 20 cm, 7 cm

Ⓒ 9 ft, 18 ft, 16 ft

Ⓓ 41 m, 40 m, 9 m

21 A total of 400 students were asked whether they prefer playing sports or watching sports. A partially completed table of relative frequencies is shown.

	Playing Sports	Watching Sports	Total
Boys		0.10	
Girls			0.60
Total	0.55	0.45	1.00

How many more boys prefer playing sports than girls?

_____

22 Which graph represents a linear function increasing at a constant rate?

Ⓐ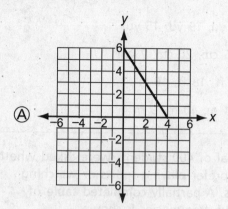

Ⓑ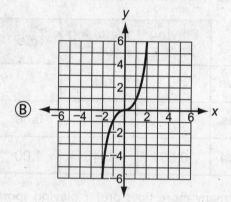

Ⓒ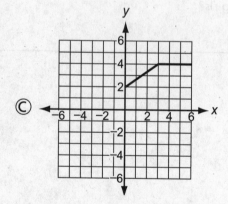

Ⓓ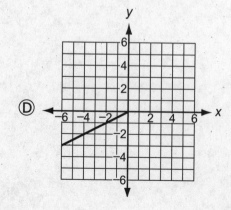

23 What is the value of x in the figure shown?

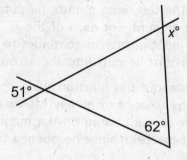

x = _____

24 The graph of a proportional relationship is shown.

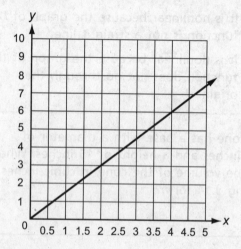

The equation $y = \frac{8}{3}x$ also represents a proportional relationship. What is the greater unit rate of the two relationships?

_____

25 Point A and point B are plotted on the coordinate plane shown.

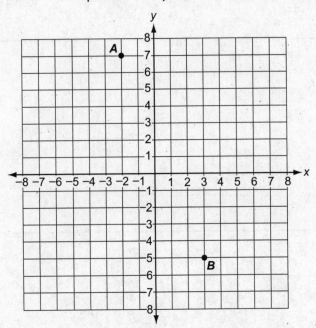

What is the distance between the two points?

(A) 5 units   (C) 13 units

(B) 12 units   (D) 17 units

26 Draw the line of best fit for the data plotted on the scatter plot shown.

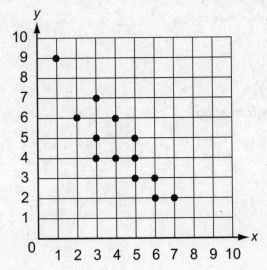

27 A cube has a volume of 0.027 cubic meter. What is the side length in meter(s) of the cube?

_____

28 Select the **three** functions that are nonlinear.

Ⓐ $y = 5^x - 7$

Ⓑ $y = 4x^3 + 9$

Ⓒ $y = -2.1x - 4$

Ⓓ $y = \frac{5}{6}x + 2$

Ⓔ $y = (2x - 1)^2$

29 A transformation is shown.

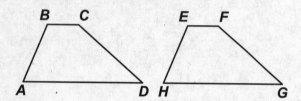

Part A

What transformation of quadrilateral *ABCD* produces quadrilateral *HEFG*?

Ⓐ horizontal translation

Ⓑ rotation about point *A*

Ⓒ dilation about point *C*

Ⓓ reflection across a vertical line

Part B

Select the **four** correct statements regarding the transformation.

Ⓐ $\overline{AB}$ is taken to $\overline{EF}$.

Ⓑ $\angle D$ is taken to $\angle G$.

Ⓒ $\overline{AD}$ is taken to $\overline{HG}$.

Ⓓ $\angle B$ is taken to $\angle F$.

Ⓔ $\overline{CD}$ is taken to $\overline{FG}$.

Ⓕ $\angle A$ is taken to $\angle H$.

30 Place an X in the table to show whether each system of equations has no solution, one solution, or infinitely many solutions.

	No Solution	One Solution	Infinitely Many Solutions
$2x = y - 4$ $y = 2x + 4$			
$y = 6(7x - 2)$ $y = 7(6x - 2)$			
$-4x + 5y = 20$ $4x + 5y = 20$			

31 The table shows the total amount, T, in dollars that Darla earns per week based on the number of overtime hours, h, she works.

Overtime Hours Worked (h)	Total Money Earned (T)
2	$860
4	$920
5	$950
8	$1,040

Which set of statements is true about this situation?

(A) The initial value is the amount of money Darla earns per week without working any overtime hours, which is $740. The rate of change is the amount of money that Darla earns per hour of overtime she works, which is $60.

(B) The rate of change is the amount of money Darla earns per week without working any overtime hours, which is $740. The initial value is the amount of money that Darla earns per hour of overtime she works, which is $60.

(C) The initial value is the amount of money Darla earns per week without working any overtime hours, which is $800. The rate of change is the amount of money that Darla earns per hour of overtime she works, which is $30.

(D) The rate of change is the amount of money Darla earns per week without working any overtime hours, which is $800. The initial value is the amount of money that Darla earns per hour of overtime she works, which is $30.

32 The equation of a function is shown.

$y = 2x + 3$

Graph the line that has the same y-intercept as the given function but has a rate of change that is two times the rate of change of the given function.

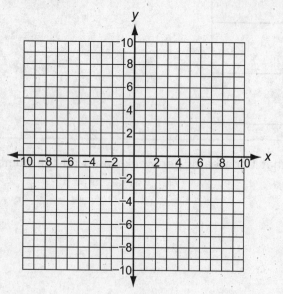

33 Which equation has no solution?

Ⓐ $5(2x - 3) = 10x - 15$

Ⓑ $-3(2x + 7) = -2(3x + 7)$

Ⓒ $-5x + 6 = -6x + 5$

Ⓓ $-6(3x - 1) = 6(-3x - 1)$

34 A bookstore receives 540 books one day. Books arrive in boxes and crates. Each box of books contains 20 books, and each crate of books contains 75 books. The bookstore received eight more boxes than crates.

• What is the total number of books that arrived in boxes that day?

• What is the total number of books that arrived in crates that day?

• Explain your reasoning and show your work.

Enter your answer and explanation in the space provided. Support your answer using words, numbers, and/or symbols.

35 The circular base of a cone has a center C. Another circle, with center B, is parallel to the base. This circle is the base of a smaller cone with height AB. Triangle ABD is similar to triangle ACE. The smaller cone is removed from Figure 1 to create Figure 2, as shown. The measurements in the diagram are given in centimeters.

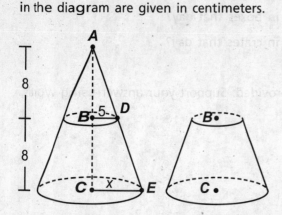

Figure 1   **Figure 2**

• What is the value of x, the radius of the larger cone?

• What is the volume of Figure 2? Round your answer to the nearest tenth.

• Explain your reasoning and show your work.

Enter your answer and explanation in the space provided. Justify your answer using words, numbers, and/or symbols.

36 The table and the graph below show Tina's and Ken's past earnings, respectively, based on the number of days worked.

Tina's Earnings

Days Worked	Earnings ($)
15	1,875
21	2,625
27	3,375

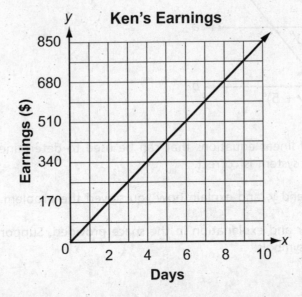

Ken's Earnings

Last year, Tina and Ken each worked a total of 20 days each month for 9 months.

Tina claims that after 5 months she earned $4,000 more than Ken. Is Tina correct? Explain why or why not.

Enter your answer in the space provided. Explain your answer using words, numbers, and/or symbols.

37 In the figure below, line *a* is parallel to line *b*. The lines are intersected by a transversal.

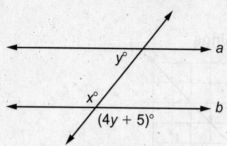

Write a system of linear equations that can be used to determine the values of *x* and *y*, and explain why your system is correct.

Then solve for *x* and *y*, and explain how you solved the problem.

Enter your answer and explanation in the space provided. Support your answer using words, numbers, and/or symbols.

38 Write one linear equation and one nonlinear equation. Explain why each equation is linear or nonlinear. Then, describe a real-world situation that can be modeled by the equation $y = 7x + 15$.

Enter your answer in the space provided. Explain your answer using words, numbers, and/or symbols.

39 Rectangle *ABCD* is shown on the coordinate plane.

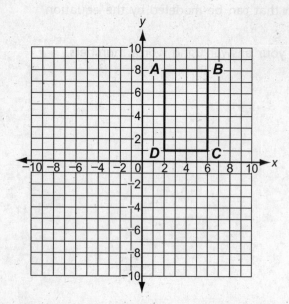

Rectangle *ABCD* undergoes a dilation, then a rotation, resulting in Rectangle *A'B'C'D'* (not shown). The length of side *A'B'* is 2 units. The coordinates of vertex *A'* are (−1, −4). The coordinates of vertex *D'* are (−6, −3).

• Describe the dilation and the rotation.

• Explain your reasoning.

Enter your answer and explanation in the space provided. Justify your answer using words, numbers, and/or symbols.